HAPPY
CHANUKAH   MATTHEW
TEVES 2 5747

LOVE,

   MUM, & DAD.

THE STORIES AND PARABLES

OF THE

Ḥafetz Ḥayyim

The Stories and Parables of the Ḥafetz Ḥayyim

gathered and arranged by
DAVID ZARETSKY

translated from the Hebrew by
CHARLES WENGROV

FELDHEIM PUBLISHERS
Jerusalem / New York

Edited by Rabbi Isaiah Aryeh Dvorkas

First published 1976
Reprinted 1980
ISBN 87306-132-2

Philipp Feldheim Inc.
96 East Broadway
New York, NY 10002

Feldheim Publishers Ltd
POB 6525 / Jerusalem, Israel

Printed in Israel

CONTENTS

II: Mitzvoth

III: The Sabbath

IV: Between man and his Maker

V: Between man and man

PREFACE

Let no one suspect me that my purpose (Heaven forbid) is to adorn myself with the mantle of the great scholars of early times, and to pretend to do what they did (in Torah study). Perish the thought! How could a poor beggar, dressed in the shabbiest rags, keeping himself alive with crumbs of bread that he collects at the homes of the wealthy, dare to go and sit among the nobility, the fine gentry of the land, fondly imagining that by sitting among them he too will be considered one of the country's noblemen? The tattered rags on his body and the collecting bag he carries will tell their own story about him, bearing witness to his dire poverty and lowly status, that make him unfit to serve even as a mat under the feet of those men of nobility.

Well, this is how I am — lowly and poverty-stricken in Torah learning and good deeds. In the Torah I know not even one halachah (definitive law) thoroughly. I haven't to my credit even one mitzvah (religious good deed) done to perfection, as we were commanded by the Divine Master of the world (blessed be His name). Then how could I ever dare pretend or imagine that what I have done is somehow similar to the achievements of those "cedars of Lebanon", the mighty giants of Torah learning whom the Lord planted among us in the early generations, long ago?

...So I have written the truth....I am only like an insignificant shammash, *a sexton, a caretaker in a* beth midrash *(house of study) who brings the great volumes by R. Isaac Alfasi and Rambam (Maimonides) to the table, so that they can be studied. Can anyone conceive that for this I should be considered their equal? Heaven forbid!*

So R. Israel Meir Hacohen, known to observant Jewry as the Ḥafetz Ḥayyim, wrote in the second Introduction to his *Likkutey Halachoth* (printed in Warsaw 1899). Through two generations this "*shammash*", this "caretaker of the *beth midrash*" kept bringing holy books to the table of Torah students in the Jewish world. Like a devoted servant, he knew where and when a particular volume would be needed. Not once was he indolent or laggard in his work; and he himself actually made the rounds, from town to town, settlement to settlement. Sometimes he rode, by train or horse-and-wagon; and sometimes he walked — through rain, snow and bitter cold. At times he went incognito, without a name; he was "just a Jew". And at times he went as "the agent of the Ḥafetz Ḥayyim", pretending that the pious sage had not come himself, but had sent him to travel about and sell his holy books and booklets. . . . To his last day he fulfilled his role as a faithful *shammash* to the Jews the world over.

For this reason not a single Jewish community was to be found anywhere within the four corners of the earth, even in the most far-flung locations, without some of the printed writings of the Ḥafetz Ḥayyim.

The last thing he wrote was *Séfer haMitzvoth haKatzér* ("The Mitzvoth in Brief"). After it was set in type, he received proofs from the printer, and found them unusually full of errors. Turning to those about him, he said, "For what purpose do I write a little volume? — so that a Jew should look into it from time to time and get to thinking — perhaps thinking about returning to better religiosity. Yet surely if this work will be so spoiled by mistakes, the reader won't understand it, and all my toil and labor will have been for nothing. So it is only right not to spare the expense, as long as a correct work comes out."

You see, whenever the Ḥafetz Ḥayyim published one of his larger or smaller volumes, he did so not because he had finished his regular work and had spare time to fill, but because the Jewish world sorely needed it. . . . His ear was turned and attuned to the pulsebeat of Jewry, and whenever he sensed the slightest spiritual lack or defect, he would immediately have a healing medicine for it in a printed message to his people. He knew that if even one important ingredient is missing in a medicine, it will not do its work — and he produced his drafts of healing words accordingly.

*   *   *

One night of Yom Kippur (the Day of Atonement), after the prayer-service, when all had gone home, the Ḥafetz Ḥayyim sat alone in the *beth midrash,* the place of Torah study and prayer. On this holiest, most solemn night of the year, he sat giving an account to his Maker of all his deeds and actions in the course of the past year. He reckoned and recalled everything, and found that there was a period of ten minutes on a certain day for which he could not account. There was no good deed that he could recall for those ten minutes. He must have frittered the time away.

At that he began weeping. "Israel Meir, Israel Meir," he admonished himself, "why did you go and waste those ten minutes on that day? The Almighty bestows His kindness on a man. He gives him a year of life, physical health, and food. The children are alive and well. But for that an account is kept there in heaven. And now the time has come to settle the account ... and ten minutes are just missing in my reckoning — gone to waste. What am I to do?" He found no answer to the question, and he wept.

With us the minutes, hours and even days can literally roll away under our feet. Whole years can roll by, cast off like refuse, without our giving them a thought, or ever having a single care. Which of us ever pays attention to a few moments that went by without Torah study? Of course there are those whose heart grieves if whole years have gone to waste and they now lie in the past like so much rubble. Some few individuals will worry in contrition over months that have sped by, wasted beyond recall. A select handful in the world may even bring to mind hours of idleness, vanished into nothing like smoke in the wind. But who in the world would ever weep over a few moments that were frittered away in the confusion of our material life? Who would even remember such moments at all?

The one who could remember such minutes had to be a man who kept the unfolding tapestry of his life spread out before him, ready to take it up in his hand and study and examine it continually, as though he were a guard of some precious treasure, appointed to watch it and be responsible for it. The only one who could pay attention to such a thing was a man who felt Heaven about him at every step he took; who did not forget for a moment that the Almighty, so to speak, was sitting with him at the table, watching everything he did, weighing and considering every move he made, counting the minutes of his day as coins from the day's earnings might be counted. The only person who could remember with such concern ten lost minutes, was one who knew that every moment for Torah study was literally as precious as a remaining moment of life for a man condemned to death — a moment that means the whole world to him.

This is why the Ḥafetz Ḥayyim was so extraordinary. And this is why he shed tears for the ten lost minutes of his life: not because he had committed any crime in that brief period (perish the thought), but simply because he could not remember what he had done with the time!

* * *

There were other great men of Torah and piety in his time. Yet he alone was singularly gifted and graced to leave his impress on his generation.

There are great Torah authorities whose supremacy rises in majesty to the very sky, like giant cypresses. Then only those with sharp vision can see the nature of the crown of learning on their heads. Others can merely see the exalted stature. On the other hand, there are great men of Torah learning who are like spreading trees with branches growing wide and far, thickly twined and leaved, to cast a pleasant shade over the wide area that they cover near the ground. Whoever wants can reach up and take some of the fruit, while he finds rest and tranquillity in the shade.

To a tree like that, many will come — old Jews, scholars, and ordinary people — to shelter in the splendid shade. Women too can find a place to rest their weary bodies; and even children can enjoy the sweet fruit, grown ripe close to the ground. Wide-spreading and lovely is the tree, providing space beneath it for all.

At times a traveler may come along, hungry and thirsty, and tired out. He can lie down to rest in the deep shade of the thick branches; and while resting, without exerting any effort, he can reach up and pick some of the fruit to refresh himself.

That was the Ḥafetz Ḥayyim for his generation. He was a giant tree in his Torah study, with the branches of his learning reaching far and wide. Yet he made sure that the branches grew low, so that everyone could reach up and benefit from them. There was hardly an observant Jew anywhere in the world, even in the most far-flung community, who did not taste and benefit, directly or indirectly, from the fruits of the Ḥafetz Ḥayyim's prolific writings.

If by chance a Jew found himself cast away in some far-off land, without any holy volumes of Torah, even without any fellow-Jews about him to talk to, he might have thought himself completely cut off from Jewry and its Torah. Yet he would have been mistaken. In Lithuania there is a small town named Radun; and there, in a little house, sat a Jew named Rabbi Israel Meir, small in height. He sat and thought of all who might become lost or banished, cast away over the seven seas — all who left their native towns and cities behind them and went wandering off across mountains, rivers and oceans....

He thought of them all, the Jews taken and tempest-tossed by the winds of new, "modern" ideologies and philosophies. And he wrote words of comfort for them: words so kind and tender and consoling, that at times you could hear an imagined echo of a mother's soothing voice. Sometimes he would scold and rebuke, yet his words of reproof were so mellow and tinged with kindness that for a moment the lost, wandering Jew could imagine it was his father sitting there and talking to comfort, encourage and guide him, scolding him a bit, but at the same time drawing out the despair from his heart; berating him a little, but at the same time leading him on a sure pathway to life.

He saw Jewish youths taken to the army. For a long time they would be torn away and separated from their homes and their neighborhoods, unable to keep the mitzvoth of the Torah. Often they would even have to desecrate the Sabbath and the festivals, in obedience to army orders. Many grieved in anxiety over the troubles of those young men. But the Ḥafetz Ḥayyim did something about it. In a special small book written for them, he gave clear instructions how they should conduct themselves in the army, in regard to the religious laws: how to be careful to remain within the code of law and avoid unnecessary violations of the Torah. With a thousand invisible threads he made them feel linked and bound with their homes, their old surroundings, the *beth midrash* where they had studied the precious pages of the Talmud.

In the knapsack of every observant soldier serving in an East European army in his time, along with his blanket, linen and tooth-brush, you could find a copy of *Maḥaneh Yisrael* by the Ḥafetz Ḥayyim.

He was a wide-spreading, thick-branched tree, making sure the fruit was in everyone's reach.

For the women there was a special place under the tree. For them this great Torah scholar wrote in a distinctive language, simple and heartwarming — so that it almost seemed to everyone reading it that a friend was talking and writing to her. It was all so clear and under-standable. . . .

For the learned student there is the order and clarity of *Mishnah B'rurah,* his unsurpassed commentary on the *Shulḥan Aruch Oraḥ Ḥayyim.* In his simple, unassuming way he showed his astonishing familiarity and brilliant grasp in the full range of authoritative re-ligious law. For the expert scholar another surprise was in store: his *Likkutey Halachoth,* written with the scope and analysis of a scholar in earlier centuries!

Simple Jews, who found their consolation in saying the prayerful words of *t'hillim* (the Book of Psalms), became his grateful students too, as they drank in the words of his *Ahavath Ḥessed.* They found new life in his *Béth Yisrael* (the House of Israel) and *Sh'mirath haLashon* (Guarding the Tongue). Where a person might find some of the points or ideas a bit difficult, there was always a little story, a homily or a parable to make it all clear. He had a way of getting home with his words, till it seemed to the reader that the booklet or book in his hands had been written just for him.

Yet in his unassuming simplicity lay the source of his greatness. For the truth is that the Ḥafetz Ḥayyim was great enough to hold the entire community of Jewry in his heart and mind.

He could reach the very depth of every Jewish spirit. He knew the ways of thought of a simple, unlettered man, just as he knew in clarity the world of the Torah scholar. His understanding of the human spirit was singularly great and profound. For this reason he became *the* pious sage of his generation. Those two simple words, *Ḥafetz Ḥayyim,* were known to every observant Jew. There was not a single religious home without some of his printed writings. He was beloved and revered by all.

For great Torah scholars, as a rule, there is reverence and respect. They are accorded honor and treated with decorum. The Ḥafetz Ḥayyim attained something more: All observant Jewry loved him. Old and young, all bore him affection....

* * *

No writer can convey in words the full greatness and holiness of the Ḥafetz Ḥayyim. Were we worthy to have him walking among us, his holy inspiring words would surely lighten the burden of misery that we carry on our bending shoulders. He always found a word of comfort for every unfortunate, embittered spirit. His hand always wiped away in compassion the tears of the poor and the lost. Were he but alive he would surely light the way for us through our physical and spiritual exile.

For this Divine kindness, however, we have not been found worthy. Our source of comfort departed this life decades ago, and his remains lie buried in the Jewish cemetery of Radun. I can but hope that the stories and parables he wrote and told in his lifetime, which in my own humble way I have managed to gather from his writings and out of my memory, as the least distinguished of his thousands of students, may evoke for us the image and spirit of our holy sage, and provide us with comfort, inspiration and guidance in our time.

David Zaretsky

I : TORAH

1
GAINING OR LOSING

Come and see how foolish those people are who make the main thing in their life the work they do for a living, and their Torah study a minor, incidental matter. They are forever busy in noisy, clamorous activity, and all their days they are occupied with nothing but the business of this world. And the main, important work, the sole purpose for which the whole world was created — that they leave in the corner.

Let us give a parable: A certain merchant constructed a large building for his business. He invested a small fortune in the building and filled it with all kinds of merchandise. Finally, though, he went and sold all the merchandise at cost price, making not a penny of profit. Then for what reason did he ever put up the building, investing all that money and effort? What was the purpose of it all?

The moral of the story is that everything has to have a purpose; everything we do must lead to something more or greater than what we started with.

Thus, to go back to our example, if a man sets himself up in business, investing thousands of dollars in it, the goal he strives for is to make more money from the business than he invested in it. If a magnificent palace is built for a mighty king, and it costs a fortune, the goal is that the powerful sovereign should dwell in it and rule his entire kingdom from there. So we see that the goal or purpose of things — the merchant's profit, and the king's royal residence in the palace — must be greater than the things themselves — the new business building or the palace.

The entire world was created for nothing but the sake of the Torah.

It is called "the beginning", and we read in Scripture, *The Lord acquired me* [the Torah] *as the beginning of His way* (Proverbs 8:22). And the Sages taught: If not for the Torah, heaven and earth would not endure; for Scripture says, *If not for My covenant* [of the Torah] *day and night, I would not have set the ordinances of heaven and earth* (Jeremiah 33:25).

So we learn that this world is only like that newly built place of business; and keeping the mitzvoth of the Torah and supporting those who learn it — that is the "profit" we can draw out from the "business" of this world. Well now, if people come along and their whole concern is only with the business itself, for its own sake, while they throw away in disdain any chance for profit — where could you find anything sillier than that?

2
THE PRECIOUS GEMS

There was once a man who conducted a large trade in diamonds and precious stones. The time came when he had to take a long trip to another country, to buy merchandise there. To make his purchases he took fifty thousand dollars, and for his traveling expenses, a thousand dollars. Once he reached his destination, he got in touch immediately with the dealers in diamonds and gems, and bought merchandise from them for the full fifty thousand dollars that he had brought. So now he was left with only 500 dollars out of the thousand for traveling expenses, having spent the other 500 to get there. His business finished, he began getting ready for the return trip.

As he left his hotel to finish up a few odds and ends before leaving the country, a man in the street stopped him. "Excuse me, sir", he said, "I was told that you are a large dealer in precious stones and diamonds. Is that true?" The dealer nodded. "Then perhaps you would be willing to buy a few things from me? I have them here with me, in my pocket. I know the worth of precious gems, and believe me, these are wonderful stones, really rare. You won't find gems like these every day. But the main thing is that you can have them for next to nothing."

"I would most certainly want to buy merchandise like that", the traveler answered. "But what can I do? I have spent all the money for merchandise that I brought with me. All I have left are a few hundred dollars for traveling expenses, so that I can get home. I don't see how I can possibly buy anything from you." Still, this man had aroused his curiosity, and he asked to see the gems which the man had called rare and wonderful.

They found a private room in the hotel, and the man took a gem case out of his pocket and opened it. The traveler could hardly believe his eyes. Stones like these came his way very infrequently. Their colors were brilliant and sparkling, and they were flawless. He simply could not take his eyes off them.

"I spoke the truth", said the other man, "didn't I? They are worth tens of thousands. I know the market value. Yet you can have them at any price you name. Business enemies of mine have brought false charges against me, and they have very good witnesses. The court will believe them. It is almost certain that the police will soon come and confiscate all my merchandise. Then I will get absolutely nothing for it. I would rather sell now what I can for any price I can get."

The traveling merchant was in a dilemma. If he bought the gems, how would he ever get home without enough money for the trip? If he didn't buy them, he would be throwing away a fabulous opportunity. He could make profit on these stones beyond all expectations. . . . He thought and thought — and reached a decision. "Look", he said, "I've left myself 500 dollars to return home by plane. If I travel by train, third class, stinting on food, I can do it for 100 dollars. So I can offer you 400 for these stones. Believe me, I would gladly give you far more if I could. They are worth a good price. But what can I do?"

Without hesitation the other accepted the offer. The merchant wrapped the case carefully and put it in a special small leather container that he strapped to his hand. Wherever he went, that case would never leave his person. Then he set off for home by train, third class.

He found himself traveling with the lowest types of menial workers and beggars. At night he slept in his seat or stretched out on the floor.

Both on the train and at stopping-off places he ate the cheapest food. And he had to keep calculating and reckoning to make sure the money left in his wallet would last till he reached his destination.

At one stop-over he spent a night in the waiting-room of the railroad station, sleeping on a bench, along with others in the room who were doing the same: beggars, mendicants and vagrants. As it happened, in the morning a wealthy diamond merchant who knew him well came in. At first he was sure he was mistaken. "Could this be you?" he asked. "What in the world are you doing here? An important dealer in precious stones like you — why didn't you spend the night in that nearby hotel? Don't tell me you have had bad luck and lost your business?"

"O no", the traveling merchant replied. "Thank Heaven, my business was never better."

"Then my good man, whatever are you doing here, pretending to be a poor beggar or something?"

The merchant took his acquaintance aside. "You know how hard a man is willing to work, how much toil and trouble he is ready to bear, to make a profit of a few thousand dollars. Here I have a chance to make a profit of at least fifty thousand." And he told the other merchant the whole story, of the opportunity that had come his way, and of the decision he had taken, so that he now had to ride home this way. With no one else watching, he carefully took out the case of gems and opened it. The other man's eyes were wide in pure astonishment.

"Well", asked the traveler, "is it not worth it for me to bear all this trouble and inconvenience now, until I get home?"

"Certainly, certainly", the other replied. "You did quite right. For a treasure like that I would be willing myself to travel home in misery. . . . There is just one thing, though, that I cannot understand. From what I remember of you, you were always a delicate and refined man. How can you withstand all that squalor and filth, and the cheap coarse food that you have to buy?"

"You may well ask", the traveler replied. "The truth is that I have been suffering indeed. I have had my fill of bad conditions on this journey. Often it becomes more than I can bear, and I almost wish myself dead and out of it, free of all the afflictions. Yet every time I am overcome by such feelings, I go off to a private corner, and with no one watching I take out the case and look at the batch of gems. I feast my eyes on their splendor, until all my burden of suffering falls away from me and I feel new strength to prevail against my dire predicament. . . . It won't last too much longer now.''

The moral of the story is that this is how every man must act whenever he wishes to acquire Torah learning and mitzvoth. Our Sages said clearly, "Such is the way of Torah study: a crust of bread with salt shall you eat, water by the small measure shall you drink, on the floor shall you sleep, a life of hardship shall you live — and in the Torah you shall toil" (Avoth vi). Which means that a man's duty is to make do with the veriest little. It may even happen at times that he will be forced to make his journey through life "homeward" as a poor, indigent beggar. He will be compelled to stay in filthy common (overpopulated) rooms, sleep on the floor, eat poor food, and generally spend his life in poverty and pressing circumstances.

Of course, when the suffering becomes too much, a man's spirit may become "fed up" with this "way of travel" through life — especially when he sees the life of affluence and ease that others live, with a beautiful home, fine clothes, good food, and so forth — things that a man's heart yearns to have.

At times like those, a man can find no better way to respond than the way of that traveling merchant. Let him take out, from time to time, the "case of precious gems", and let him "feast his eyes on their brilliance and luster" — meaning the precious jewels and gems of Torah learning and mitzvoth that became his for "a very low price", but particularly by virtue of his willingness to make do with little, in return for the hard life that he has been willing to bear.

For this world is only in the nature of a corridor, a "way home" along which we travel. So we can travel through it under distressing difficulties, in order to gain afterward that "great profit" upon reaching our true "home" — the world-to-come, which is in the nature of a mansion. When we consider that reward against the life of penury, we will see at the end, that it was really a good "business deal", and our mind will be at rest.

3
A TIME OF OPPORTUNITY

When the years go by in order, peace reigns among nations, and there is tranquillity in the world, it is very hard for a plain soldier to go up the ladder of promotion rapidly and become a high-ranking officer. He will have to spend many years in the army, and excel in various courses of study and kinds of duty. We will hardly ever see a *young* man succeed in reaching a high officer's rank in the army, or in the government either; for by and large, only men of more advanced age, with established reputations, are appointed to such positions.

In a time of war, however, when the country and its people are in peril, even young people can reach a high, prestigious rank by exposing themselves to danger and doing acts of heroism that help bring victory over the enemy, or other acts of great benefit to the country. When the perils of war are over, and the population has overpowered the enemy and driven it out of the land, the king (or president, or prime minister) will recall gratefully all those whose valor helped save the country from danger. He will then honor and exalt them, and he may also appoint them to important positions, raising them to high rank as army officers. Thus in a time of crisis a young man may also achieve a high position by virtue of his actions.

Well, it is the same in Torah study. In olden times, when the world of Jewry was replete with Torah learning, there were numerous great scholars, valiant pastors of our flocks, sound men with a reverent fear of Heaven. Those times were in the nature of periods of peace, when the years go by in order; and it was difficult then for an ordinary man to rise to the rank of a great, noble authority in Torah. A vast amount of Torah learning was necessary, to be gained only through years of toil and wearying diligence.

In our times, though, it is different. It is now a time of crisis for us. The students of Torah are few in number. As for great scholars and authorities, a child can count them. Now it is not hard at all for even an ordinary person, through assiduous application and strong effort, to attain the rank of a great prince of Torah learning, becoming close to Him, be He blessed.

This is something a person must always bear in mind, so that he will not let his time of opportunity slip by.

4

LIKE TRYING TO GET BLOOD

How many days slip away from us without any Torah study, filled instead with idle matters. We hardly sense or pay any attention how time gets frittered away, without any study of Torah, which is our life and the length of our days. We invest all our interest and energy in the affairs of this world — for example, how to earn a great deal of money; and we fondly imagine that this money we gather will stand by us in a time of need, and we will even be able to save our lives with it.

If that is what we think, we are sadly mistaken.

Let us give a parable to explain: The only son of a rich man took sick and was confined to bed. Looking at him, you could not tell at all that he was ill. He looked fine. Yet he felt wretchedly sick, and he hadn't the strength to stand on his feet.

Doctors came and examined him, and they said they found no particular disease or ailment. The boy was only suffering from a severe lack of blood in his system. For this there was no medicine whatever, but only one way of cure: to inject a large amount of blood into the boy's body. This was, however, before the time of blood donors and blood banks, and there was only one thing the doctors could suggest: to find a way to draw the needed large amount of blood out of someone's healthy body. Once the transfusion was done, said the doctors with complete certainty, the boy would recover.

The wealthy father left the house and went to the very poorest people in the town. "I am ready to put down any amount of money you want", he said. "Only let me draw out a large measure of blood from one of your children, so that it can be injected into the body of my child. He is desperately ill, and this is the only way to make him well."

The poor people looked at him thoughtfully. They were no fools, and they knew that if a large amount of blood was taken from any child's body, that child was virtually certain to die. "We are sorry, sir", they answered. "For this kind of money that you offer, we are ready and willing to do any kind of work or task in the world. We will take risks. But to give you a child of ours to take out his blood and give it to you to cure your son — that we cannot do. Blood is the very life of a human being, the source of his vitality. How can we expose the life of a child of ours to almost certain death, just for the payment of money?"

The Torah is our matrix of life. From it we draw our spiritual vitality. Without Torah learning we can be compared to a dried-up tree whose source of water is depleted, so that its leaves must wither. We become like a living creature whose source of fresh blood is gone. And thus we are in great danger of being left without an ounce of spiritual strength.

So people come along and say, "We have an answer: We will take the money we saved up in the days we spent without Torah study, and give it to Torah scholars. In that way we can purchase from them a share of the reward they have earned for learning Torah." How can anyone imagine that some person will ever be found who is willing to sell for money the source of his spiritual life? About this we can quote Solomon, the wisest of men, *If a man would give all the wealth of his house for love, he would be utterly scorned* (Song of Songs 8:7).

For this reason a man has to think the matter over carefully and try with all his might to set fixed, specific times for Torah study as long as he is able to, so that his spirit will not be left lacking this main source of its life and vitality.

5
NOT ALL THE SHARES ARE ALIKE

The Ḥafetz Ḥayyim was once asked: For whatever reason is such

a great big commotion made about idling away time without Torah
study? Why do the rabbis and Torah instructors raise a hue and cry
about it to the very heavens? Our Sages clearly teach, "All Jews have
each a share in the world-to-come" (Mishnah, Sanhedrin x 1). Then
why all the furor because there are some people who have no fixed,
regular time for Torah study?

The Ḥafetz Ḥayyim answered thoughtfully:

Let me tell you a story: In Kiev, in former times, there was a very
wealthy man named Brodsky. He owned a considerable number of
factories, that employed thousands of employees: ordinary workers,
skilled craftsmen, and clerks; and among them there were many relatives of his: close kin and distant relations. A few of these relatives,
unable to do any useful work, received a salary nevertheless, in return
for nothing, so that it was really a monthly allowance.

One fine day Brodsky decided to visit one of his factories, to see
how the work was getting on there, and to see if the workers and
their foremen seemed both satisfied and satisfactory. The officials of
the factory took him through all the rooms and departments, and they
had all the workers come forward to meet him; whereupon he would
ask each in turn what he did, how much he was paid, whether he
was content with his work, and so on.

Among all the employees there was one who could give only a
single brief answer to the owner's questions. Brodsky wanted to know
where in the factory he worked, what kind of tasks he performed,
and how much he received. His only answer was, "There is a fixed
salary that I receive every month." Of course, although he said it
with as much dignity as he could muster, he meant that he was only
one of the "relatives", receiving his pay for sitting idle and producing
nothing.

We can well imagine how chagrined and ludicrous he looked at
that moment, having to let Brodsky and all the people with him
realize clearly that he merely received a monthly "hand-out".

It is true, beyond any doubt, that as the Sages taught, "all Jewry
have each a share in the world-to-come"; but what a great difference
it will make whether a person works for it in this world and earns

it as his rightful reward, or he is to receive it as a "hand-out", like Brodsky's relative.

6

THE NEED TO MOBILIZE

Even when the times are in order and peace reigns, every country always maintains a standing army, staffed by soldiers who are found fit for military duty, being strong and without any ailments or handicaps. They serve for a fixed period, and having finished their army service they return home to live a civilian life.

In times of danger, however, when an enemy stands at the gates threatening to invade and capture the country, so that no one's life is safe, everybody is then mobilized into the army. There is a general call-up into the fighting forces. Everyone goes, even those who would be exempt from army duty in peacetime. Every man has to do what he can, and even more. A person who can handle a weapon goes to the fighting lines. A person who cannot, works in various other branches or departments of the military operation. There are some who are drafted to teach military strategy and ways of battle, this being one of the most important ways of serving in a time of war.

Apart from all this, though, the heads of governmental branches and of the armed forces meet to plan and find ways to increase the country's military readiness. They check if there is enough ammunition, equipment and food in reserve to conduct the war, which could well continue for a long time.

For our many sins, the times we live in have become in the nature of a period of peril and crisis, with a harsh enemy at our gates about to attack, threatening our very existence. The power and dominion of the evil inclination have increased to a frightening extent. It continues to drive ever more people into defiance and rebellion against the Divine King of kings, the Holy Blessed One, and His holy Torah.

So a sacred duty lies on every Jew in the Torah world, from the great scholar and authority to the lowest student in the yeshivoth, to form and join an "armed force" for the honor of the Lord, to go out and battle this enemy that has arisen against us to make an end of us. If we will not do everything in our power to vanquish it, the danger looms that this enemy will conquer our final defenses; and then who knows if we will ever succeed in regaining the upper hand?

It is therefore the obligation of our rabbis and great Torah luminaries to gather and devise plans and strategy for conducting this war. They must investigate if the weapons and soldiers at our disposal are enough for this armed conflict; or if there is a need to muster more soldiers out of the holy herds of our Torah students. It is for anyone and everyone imbued with the spirit of Torah, to enroll in the ranks at once. Whoever knows the Hebrew Scriptures, let him teach the Scriptures to study groups. Whoever knows the Mishnah, let him teach the Mishnah; if one knows religious law, let him teach that to study groups. In this way we will increase the various kinds of weapons and armaments with which we can go to war.

Whoever is greater than his neighbor has a greater duty toward his people. It is his duty to assemble groups of Jews and upbraid and criticize them in rebuke, to bring them back completely to the good path, by showing them the way of repentance and return that they must take. The main thing, though, is to keep a watchful eye on our most vital defense-line: the little school-children — to make sure they are reared in Torah study and holiness.

This is the only way to overcome our great enemy in this difficult battle.

7

THE EMERGENCY INJECTION

When blood courses through a person's veins, it is a sign that the person is alive; and the nature of his pulse is an indication of his state of health. If the pulse is in order, firm and regular in its beat, it means the man is well. If it races too fast or beats too slowly, it is a sign that the man's state of health is out of order, and a doctor must be called in to treat him.

Once a sick person grew very feeble. A group of doctors was hastily called to examine him, with a noted professor at their head. They examined the patient carefully and found various wounds and defects in his limbs. As a result they decided to prepare special bandages for the injured limbs.

As they were attending him, though, the professor noticed that the patient's blood pressure had fallen dangerously low. He turned to his colleagues and students, the doctors who had come with him to examine the patient. "Gentlemen", said he, "this is not the time to discuss and consider which bandage will be most effective for the patient. His blood pressure has fallen so low that there is immediate danger to his life. We must give him an injection at once to raise the pressure. Otherwise I'm afraid there will be no need to treat his injured limbs any more!"

The Almighty's Torah is the blood that courses through our veins. It gives us spiritual life, and remains a sure sign of our spiritual health. If the sound of Torah learning is heard in our schools, it indicates that the circulation in our spiritual veins and arteries is in order. If, however, the sound of Torah learning grows feeble, it is a clear sign that we are mortally sick, and nothing will save our spiritual life except an injection to restore the circulation to normal — an injection of our holy Torah.

Every one of us must therefore know that we have to watch properly over the voices of Torah learning: to make sure they are heard resounding everywhere, at every time. As we strengthen our forces in the study of Torah and the observance of its mitzvoth, we will save our spiritual life and assure our continued existence.

8
THEY IGNORE THE MAIN PURPOSE

Every act that a person does has its own end-purpose; and the end-purpose indicates how important the act or action is. Moreover, the one who does the act will also be an indication of how important it is.

When a man opens a new store (shop), having invested in it a tremendous amount of work and expenses, he is hopeful that the store will support him and his family. Thus the thought behind his action is revealed by the purpose it shows, which means the expected results of his activity. For he clearly opened his store in order to be able to support his family.

If we see a worthy man of distinction engaged in some risky activity, we will have no doubt that his action must be of considerable importance, and it will bring results accordingly. If a mighty emperor has a splendid palace built for him, costing heavy millions, he will most certainly establish there, in full pomp and majesty, the seat of his empire.

Well, if this is the rule among us mortals of flesh and blood, it must certainly apply then to even the simplest act of the Almighty (if we may so speak), and how much more certainly when an important activity of His is involved.

Now, here the Almighty Himself, in all His majesty, created heaven and earth and everything in them. What was the end-purpose of this great act of creation? — the study of our holy Torah. For our Sages taught: *In the beginning God created* (Genesis 1:1) — for the sake of the Torah, that is called "the beginning", as Scripture says, *The Lord acquired me* [the Torah] *as the beginning of His way* (Proverbs 8:22). And it says further, *If not for My covenant* [of the Torah] *day and night, I would not have set the ordinances of heaven and earth* (Jeremiah 33:25).

Clearly the Torah is the end-purpose of the entire creation.

Then woe to those people without sense whose evil inclination lures them into reducing the time of Torah study for themselves and even for their children, so that they can devote ever more time for business and trade. They abandon the key purpose, the Torah, in which the true good and eternal existence lie implicit, through which a man becomes worthy to find eternal pleasure in the company of the Divine King of glory. The result is that these people treat the Torah not as the main purpose but as something trivial and inconsequential. How terribly shameful it is!

9

STAMPED WITH THE TORAH'S SEAL

During the First World War the Russian army employed thousands of technicians and craftsmen with various skills, to work for the armed forces. In return, these people were free of military duty.

Of course, every craftsman and technician received from the army all the materials that he needed for his work. But to make it clear to all that each man was working for the army, all the materials for him would be stamped with the official seal of the Russian army.

In the course of a conversation someone told the Ḥafetz Ḥayyim of this. "Oh", he replied, "it is quite the same with labor for the Almighty. If they come and ask a shoemaker why he is not serving in the army he can take out the military boots and rubbers that he is making, with the army seal stamped on the leather. 'You see', he will say, 'I am already enrolled in the army, since I am working for it. This is my way of doing military service.'

"Well, it is the same in regard to serving the Lord. If a shoemaker or carpenter who is busy at his work all day should be asked, 'But what will become of the Torah in your life? Why don't you busy yourself with Torah study the entire day?' — he can answer, 'When I carry the burden of earning a living, how can I busy myself with Torah study? I have to support a wife and children. I have to pay for the education in Torah that my children receive. And I support yeshivoth (Torah schools) so that the Torah should not be forgotten in Jewry. For this reason I have no time left to learn it properly myself.'

"So we see that since the shoemaker or carpenter is working all day so that his children can learn Torah and he can help maintain yeshivoth, the seal of the holy Torah is stamped on his handiwork. He is really also working for the Almighty in his daily occupation.

"In this regard Scripture says, *In all your ways, know Him* (Proverbs 3:6). In other words every Jew has a duty to make a reckoning about the life he is living, to see that all the roads he takes and follows should be in accord with a knowledge or awareness of the Lord — that his main work should be stamped with the seal of the Torah and the reverent fear of Heaven; with the purpose of giving his children an education to learn the Torah and cling firmly to it. Then all his labor will indeed be stamped with the Torah's seal."

10
FEW BUT PRECIOUS

A farmer once came to the big city, to visit a friend. The friend, who had been living in the city a long time, took him through the streets to show him the sights: beautiful houses, landscapes, and so forth.

At first they came to a street with large, wholesale places of business. They saw huge buildings where grain and produce were sold wholesale, in large quantity, to fruit-and-vegetable dealers. The farmer was impressed. He saw whole lofts in warehouses filled to the brim with sacks of wheat and flour. He saw crates of fruit, barrels of oil, casks of sugar, and so on.

When he had seen his fill, the two went on till they reached the textile market. Here the places of business were not so large; and the shelves that filled the stores were not stocked to the brim. The stores that dealt in fine silk were still smaller, and their quantity of materials rather limited. The farmer noted everything carefully, appreciating the fine quality of the goods; and then the two continued on their way.

In another part of town they found silversmiths and dealers in silverware. Here the stores were quite small, containing only two or three cases that displayed the fine objects of silver. Among the goldsmiths and dealers in precious stones, a store generally contained only one case, showing perhaps a few watches and some pieces of jewelry, set with precious gems and diamonds. Thus most of a store like that was simply empty space.

When the farmer returned home, he told his rustic friends of all the wonderful, impressive things he had seen in the big city. He described the huge lofts and warehouses of the grain and produce merchants. Then he told of the stores in the textile market, amply filled with shelves of all kinds of knit and woven cloth; but, he added, in the silk stores there was not too much merchandise at all. There he was not impressed Then he went on to describe his utter astonishment at the last stores he had seen: the business quarters of the silversmiths and goldsmiths, and the dealers in gems and precious stones. Why, he said, there was almost nothing in those shops. Even the general store in their local village had more wares than that. He just could not understand, he said, how little shops like those ever came to be in such a fine big city.

Well, a visitor from the city happened to be sitting there, listening, and he burst out laughing: "If that isn't the silliest thing I ever heard", he guffawed. "You poor country boob! Don't you understand that the cheaper, common wares are always found in large quantities? On the other hand, gold, silver and precious jewels are rare. There is only a small quantity of them in the world. So they are very expensive; and it is impossible for one dealer to fill up his whole store with them — even a little shop. You should realize that one little pearl may be worth more than thousands of sacks of flour!"

So very many have complained and bemoaned the fact that (for our numerous sins) the number of students and supporters of Torah learning keeps growing smaller and smaller. As a result, they add, the number of great Torah scholars is likewise dwindling; and who knows where it will all end? How will we stand before the blessed Lord on judgment day, empty-handed, with no answer to give for the fate of Torah study in our generation?

The truth of the matter, though, is not like that at all. Since the number of Torah students in our time has grown so small, they are like precious jewels in Heaven's eyes. Each one is like a golden ornament inlaid with precious stones; their worth is very great. In the eyes of the blessed Lord, every one of them is equal in value to thousands upon thousands of ordinary people, who fill whole regions of this world from brim to brim.

11

A SQUINT-EYED VISION OF THE TORAH

A mighty emperor once built an entire fortified area for his royal seat of government. There he constructed many splendid mansions and palaces for himself, and large imposing edifices for his royal officers, counsellors and servants. The entire group of buildings was constructed of hewn stone, and the structures rose tall and solid.

Great windows in all the palaces allowed the king to look out over the whole area, and beyond it across the entire capital city.

One day a squint-eyed man, who saw everything crooked, came walking by this fortified royal area. Unfortunately, he knew nothing at all about his defective eyesight, which had gone bad only recently, and he thought his vision was normal. He looked up at the tall, majestic buildings, and they all seemed crooked, leaning dangerously and about to collapse. The thick wall that surrounded the entire area looked likewise crooked and leaning perilously outward. In fact, all the buildings in the capital seemed to be standing at a tilt, their roofs perilously at the side. At any moment, he was sure, everything would come crashing down in a great collapse, leaving only piles of rubble with all the people there buried underneath.

With all his might he began running through the streets of the city, to save himself from the disaster; and as he ran he shouted at the top of his lungs, "Hurry, save yourselves! Get away from this terrible place! In another minute all these buildings will come crashing down and bury you alive. Hurry, get out of here as fast as you can, before it is too late!"

The people all about looked up with their healthy eyesight, and saw that all the buildings were standing sound and proper. How could those edifices fall? So they laughed at the man. Either he was perpetrating a practical joke, they thought, or else he had lost his reason. There were a few silly souls among them, however, easily frightened, and the man's shouts and screams cast a spell of terror over them. They could pay no attention to the words of reason by the sane, understanding people around them, who laughed in scorn at all the warnings of the squint-eyed man. Those poor silly souls picked up their legs and began running in utter confusion through the streets of the city, convinced that they had to save themselves because the buildings were really on the verge of falling.

With all their strength the unruffled sober people tried to stop them and calm them down. "You dithering idiots", they said. "Lift up your eyes and see how strong and solid those buildings are. What are you running from? Go and look at the king and his officers. You don't see *them* running wildly through the streets. They are staying, calm and peaceful, in their mansions and palaces. And what of their numerous servants and attendants? They are also going peacefully about the palace buildings, doing their work calmly and serenely. It has not occurred to any of them to think that this magnificent group of buildings is about to collapse. Then what are you alarmed about? Why has all this terror driven you out of your wits, just because of what a man with crooked eyesight said? Think about it for a moment, and stop this agitated stupid running!"

Yet the wise people could achieve nothing with their words. The foolish men continued running as though berserk. Their eyes filled with terror, they ran with all their strength, shouting, "Hurry! Save yourselves, everybody! The buildings are falling!"

Suddenly one clever man stepped out in front of the fleeing mob and raised his voice above all the tumult and confusion: "A doctor! Hurry and bring a doctor, quickly!"

In puzzlement, the fleeing people stopped. "A doctor?" they asked. "What good will a doctor do here? Can a doctor bring some medicine to heal the damage in all these buildings?"

"No, no", said the clever man. "That is not what I had in mind at all. It is not to shore up those buildings that I need a doctor. They are strongly built, to last. I want a doctor in order to cure that man of his squint. Once he can see straight, he will convince the other fools who have senselessly followed him that the buildings are all standing solidly on their foundations and are not about to collapse at all. He will realize that his vision was distorted because he suffered from a squint, and this made him see everything at a slant, leaning over.

The moral of the story is as simple as can be.

Our holy Torah is a fortified castle, the special area of the Divine King of the world, that He created and built. There are, however, sick people stricken with defective, distorted vision, and it seems to them that this castle is about to collapse (Heaven forbid); it is not standing on a solid foundation. So they are fleeing at great speed to escape from it to safety. However, those people who are blessed with clear vision and a steady mind scorn and jeer at these persons with crooked sight: "You squint-eyed donkeys! Stop spouting such non-sense. How do you dare say that a mighty structure like that is going to collapse? Only your own half-blindness could have put such a lunatic idea into your heads. This building is strong and sound, built to last forever!"

12
THE EMPTIED ARSENAL

Two kings of neighboring countries were forever at war with each other; and their hostilities never ended with a decisive victory. Some-times one side won, sometimes the other.

On either side they turned the matter over in their minds, con-sidering it from every aspect, and they came to the conclusion that with the kind of warfare they conducted, their battles would never be ended. The counsellors of both kings met to find some plan that could be followed; and they decided to suggest to both kings to set a fixed, limited amount of time for continuing the war. Whichever side would succeed in winning by the end of this set period would be considered the victor in the war.

The two kings accepted the plan, and they agreed that the fighting should go on for another four days. Whichever side was winning on the fourth day would be declared victorious.

On the first day the forces of the first king scored triumphs. On the second day, the other king's army gathered its strength and made gains on its enemy. The third day, the first king's forces fought strongly and prevailed again. In the evening the generals of that army met to decide on some strategy that would make them win against the enemy the next day also, so as to become the victors of the entire war.

One of the generals began: "Gentlemen, tomorrow is the day of decision. Tomorrow will decide if we triumph or go down in complete defeat. If we do not win the battle on this coming day, all our efforts, all our gains and victories in battles till now will have been in vain. All the sacrifices we have made will be for nothing. Yet we know that yesterday our enemy gained the upper hand; and who knows if they won't be too much for us again tomorrow?

"Now this is what I propose we do: The spies that I sent into the enemy camp have returned with good news. They found the ammunition supplies of the enemy. We now know where they keep all their stocks of weapons and munitions. And the most important thing I have learned is that this arsenal is not heavily guarded at all. They have only a few soldiers watching it. Let us send over a few of our best soldiers, strong and courageous men. Some of our spies who know the enemy territory will go along to show them the way. They will put the enemy guards out of the way, capture all the ammunition, and bring it over to our side, in carefully prepared transport. Let this plan succeed, and we will know we cannot lose!"

All the generals there agreed to the plan enthusiastically; and they lost no time in carrying it out. A group of fearless, valiant fighters were sent over in the dark of night into the enemy camp, and they did their work swifty and efficiently. Whatever they could carry, they took out of the enemy's supply depot to their waiting vehicles. Whatever they could not take with them, they destroyed, to make sure it would be of no further use to the foe. Their work at the supply depot done, they sped back through the night into their own camp.

As dawn rose, trumpets sounded to herald the start of the final battle, that would decide the long-standing war. The second side was well rested and fiercely determined. Having lost yesterday, they were resolute in their readiness to fight tooth and nail for the final, decisive victory. Soldiers were despatched at double speed to bring up weapons and fresh ammunition.

Soon, however, they learned the terrible news: Their sentries had been killed or knocked unconscious, and their ammunition supply was completely gone. Fiercely ready for battle as they were, they would do no fighting that day. With sinking hearts they ran up the white flag of surrender.

As long as a person is alive on earth, he is in constant battle with the evil inclination. It devises all kinds of schemes and stratagems not to let a Jew study Torah, observe its mitzvoth, do good deeds, or worship and serve the blessed Lord with all his heart. It is of necessity a long and difficult war, but (thank Heaven) the evil inclination does not always gain the upper hand. At times the Jew prevails, and he succeeds in fighting free from the grip of the "other (satanic) side", to be able to purify himself and draw closer to the blessed Lord. Alas, though, at other times it happens that (Heaven spare us) the evil inclination is victorious; and then the Jew draws further away from the Divine source of the spirit.

At last the "other side" sees that this is going to be a protracted war, a long-drawn-out affair with no end in sight. By the ordinary methods of warfare that he uses, he will never be certain of a complete, decisive victory. So Satan makes up his mind to use a cunning, treacherous trick: He will bother and distract the Jew so as to prevent him from learning any Torah. In that way he will steal away from him his main weapon and ammunition, especially the shield that has always guarded and protected him in battle. Once that is done, Satan's complete victory is assured. Without the merit of Torah, how can a Jew survive in his battle with the evil inclination?

Every Jew must therefore keep well in mind that the main thing is Torah learning. That is his chief armor, the shield that protects him in his battle with the evil impulse. As long as we still have this in our arsenal, we can withstand the onslaughts of the battle, even if the fighting becomes thick and fierce and it continues long without a let-up, and it often even seems that the "other (evil) side" is winning. But how very, very great and fearful is the danger of a downfall (Heaven spare us) when we are devoid and empty of Torah learning and mitzvoth; when our arsenal is completely empty, with not a bit of armor or a weapon to defend us. How are we ever to stand in battle with no ammunition whatever in our hands?

13
THE EXCHANGE THAT WAS REFUSED

If you met an observant Jew on the street and asked him, "Tell me: do you know how great a mitzvah (a religious good deed) it is to learn Torah? And do you know what dire punishment awaits those who can learn it and don't?" — he would very probably answer, "O, certainly I know."

Then you might ask, "In that case, please explain why there is such a widespread neglect and avoidance of Torah study in our time!"

Well, the matter can be understood by a parable:

In a certain country the time came for a new king to ascend the throne and rule the land. The royal officers met and decided that, in honor of his coronation, they would surprise the king by having a new handsome crown made for him. They made inquiries far and wide, and learned that in one particular town there was an unusually gifted craftsman in gold and silver, who was well-suited to the task of making the new crown. He could be trusted to produce something really fine and splendid.

Losing no time, they sent two officers to him, to bring him a large amount of gold metal and precious gems. The craftsman set to work and fashioned a beautiful royal crown out of the gold, and into it he set the diamonds and precious stones. When it was finished, he gave it to the two officers.

As they saw, the work was really exquisite. It was more beautiful than anything they had ever seen. Wrapping it carefully, they set off to return to the capital city.

On the way they passed through towns and villages, forests and fields. They saw peasants at work, plowing their land. Said one officer to the other, "Do you want to see something very interesting? You won't believe your eyes and ears."

"All right", said the other. "Show me. I want to see."

The first officer stopped their horse-drawn coach and called over a few peasants from the fields. "Do you want to see something very beautiful that we have with us?" he asked them. "Yes indeed", they replied. "Let us see." The officer took out the crown from its wrapper and let them gaze their fill. They were deeply impressed. "That is a wonderful thing", said one of them. "I don't think we have ever seen anything so lovely in our lives."

"Well", said the officer, "maybe you would like to make an exchange. Come: I will give you this crown, and you will give me for
it a pair of oxen, that you use to plow the field. Does any one of you
want to make the exchange?"

One farmer stepped forward: "All right. I like the idea. Done —
just as you say. Let us swap."

"What is the matter with you?" another farmer blurted out. "What
kind of foolishness are you going to do? How can you make such
a mistake? With your pair of oxen you plow your field, so that you
can plant your wheat and grow your crop. That is how you support
yourself and your family. What are you going to do with that crown?
It certainly is lovely; but can you plow your field with it?"

And that was how the matter ended. The first farmer withdrew
his consent, whereupon the officers wrapped up the crown and rode
off.

For a long time they could hardly stop laughing. "What stupid
yokels", said one to the other. "For any small part of the crown,
even the smallest, they could get enough money to buy a hundred
pairs of oxen. If they only knew what a royal crown like this is
worth — a thousand times more than all their fields and forests!"

Now, could not most people be compared to those peasants and
farmers?

They certainly know that the Torah is a precious, lovely possession,
a treasure beyond all wisdom. When the good inclination comes and
tells them to gain some knowledge of it, they agree at once. The
radiance of the Torah brings light to their eyes, and they long for its
splendor. Yet along comes the satanic scoundrel, the evil inclination,
and starts arguing: "You blessed fools! In the time that you spend
studying Torah you could be engaged in business, buying and selling.
You could be out in the world of commerce making so much money
— and money is the answer to everything, you know."

Without thinking, the people are persuaded by the lures of the evil
inclination. They refuse to barter a pair of oxen for a royal crown. . . .

14

THE MOST PROFITABLE MERCHANDISE

A wise man knows how much good reward awaits him in the world-to-come (the Afterlife) for every mitzvah. He knows how to calculate and value the reward set for every religious good deed. And for this reason he makes every effort and tries with all his ability to keep as many mitzvoth as he can.

Truth to tell, this is the way of all people in the world. Every tradesman and shopkeeper keeps an account of what he buys and sells, always making a reckoning of how much he has earned. And so he tries to do as much buying and selling as he can.

A small tradesman, who does not sell much merchandise, will yet write down in his account book that these and these goods brought him so much profit. The profit is certainly little (since he does a small amount of business). Nevertheless he writes it down, so that he will remember that it is worthwhile for him to buy more of it.

A man with a larger store or shop, where more customers come to buy, is sure to mark down larger profits in his account book. And we may be sure that he will not trouble himself to deal in merchandise that brings in very little profit.

Now, just think for yourself: If an overseas trading company deals in some merchandise, importing it from India and selling it wholesale, in large quantities, to storekeepers all over the country — when that company makes a reckoning of its profit on the merchandise, it must surely run to thousands of dollars at least. Otherwise it would not pay for such a large company to deal in the merchandise.

Well, let us stop and consider: The blessed Lord is the Divine King of the world. The entire world is His "place of business", if we may so speak. In His heavenly account book, where His "business dealings" with every human being are recorded, it is noted that the Torah is the very best and finest merchandise, worth far more than the most precious rubies and pearls. Then the profit to be made on this merchandise must certainly be far more than anything that can be earned on other goods and wares — infinitely more — so that no earthly fortune can compare to it.

Who earns this profit? — any "tradesman" shrewd enough to "buy" a knowledge of the Torah by studying it regularly. So we would all do well to remember how to appreciate and value the Torah, a source of incomparable "profit" in the Hereafter.

15
REASON TO REGRET

There was once a very wealthy man who came to be. hated by vindictive business enemies. Off they went to the officials of the government treasury and lodged a complaint against him that he manufactured counterfeit money. As evidence they produced a few forged bank notes (pieces of paper money), insisting that they had received them from this wealthy man.

This was not a country that gave every accused citizen a fair trial, believing him innocent until he would be proven guilty. Instead, the wealthy man was arrested and put in prison for a long time, where he was subjected to severe physical torture, to make him confess to his "crime". Yet, being strong in spirit, he refused to confess to something he had not done. Finally the judges decided to subject him to torture once more, but this time publicly, in the city square. Then he was to be banished to a slave-labor camp in a far-off province, where he was to work at hard labor for the rest of his life.

When he was brought in chains to the city square, to be put to torture, a great crowd quickly assembled to watch the sight. The judges sat in their places of honor on the dais, and the prison guards stood in position, as the prisoner was brought up on the dais, his hands and feet bound in irons.

Among the people watching, there happened to be another man of great wealth, who knew the prisoner very well and was also on friendly terms with many government officials. In fact, his business often took him to the courts of justice, and he knew a good many judges quite well.

As soon as he recognized his good friend, standing there in chains like some hardened criminal, he was overwhelmed with astonishment. He could hardly believe his eyes. He had known this man for years, and the man had always been honest and honorable. He was certain the man was innocent, and some terrible mistake had been made.

Without hesitation he went up on the dais and spoke to the presiding judge, whom he knew: "Excuse me, your honor. Could you please tell me for what crime this man was sentenced?"

"He printed counterfeit paper money."

"That is impossible. I cannot believe it. I have known this man well for a good number of years, and I have always found him honest and trustworthy. I have met few people as honorable as he. He would never stoop to dealing in counterfeit money. I can guarantee you, your honor, that there has been some mistake here. Your honor can inquire and investigate about him among the people in his town. They will all tell you the same thing about him."

Impressed by these strong words, the presiding judge had the prisoner taken back to his cell, and he sent for a large number of people from the man's town. All without fail testified that he was honest and trustworthy, and it was out of the question to think he would print counterfeit bills.

At last the judges gave their decision: "We realize that the matter is not as we believed at first. Nevertheless, we are not entirely convinced that the man is altogether innocent, since there is evidence that counterfeit bills were received from him. It is therefore our decision to lighten his sentence: He will be free from any further torture, in secret or in public. He will not be sentenced to hard labor in the distant province. Yet he cannot be let off scot-free. It is our verdict that he must go from here to live in a distant town. He will be free to move about in the town and do as he pleases there; but for the rest of his life he will be forbidden to leave it."

It can be imagined how happy the prisoner was to hear what a light sentence he received, after the fate that had hung over his head. He was sent off immediately to some far-off town in the land, and there he made his home.

Time went by, and as luck would have it, his friend who had recognized him in the city square, when he was about to be tortured in public, happened to come to this far-off town. Going at once to visit him, to his surprise the friend found him sitting sad and dejected, under a cloud of deep melancholy. As soon as the ex-prisoner saw his friend, however, he jumped up and shook his hand warmly, as tears stood in his eyes. "Welcome, welcome", he said. "It is so good of you to come and visit me. How can I ever thank you enough for the great kindness you did for me? You saved me from torture and from a life of hard, cruel labor."

"O, it was nothing", said the other. "What is a friend for if not to help in a time of need? But tell me: If you know and appreciate how very much better it turned out, compared to the fate that awaited you before I came along, why are you so sad and dejected, wallowing in sorrow and despair? You should always be happy and cheerful that you were saved from the prison cell and the slave-labor camp!"

"That is true", said the man. "You are perfectly right. Yet I keep remembering all that I had before this terrible thing happened to me. I was wealthy. I conducted a thriving business. I was respected and honored by my townspeople. Relatives and friends would always come to visit me, and I would go to visit them. Now I am under orders to remain here, in this town, till my last day on earth — far from my dearest relations and friends. Here I must end my days on earth, alone and forgotten. How can I remember all that and still be happy?"

This is what Scripture means when it says, *But I returned and regarded ... and behold, the tears of the oppressed, and they had no one to comfort them* (Ecclesiastes 4:1). As Rashi notes, it refers to the wicked who suffer in purgatory. This is what Solomon, the wisest of men, means by it: When people have sinned during their life on earth, then even after they have been punished enough and the demons no longer have any right to punish them and afflict them with pain and suffering, they nevertheless continue to shed tears and weep: not because of the pain of afflictions, but for the simple reason that they have no Torah learning and mitzvoth to their credit, in which they can take comfort and solace for their anguished, wretched spirit.

While they were alive they could have acquired as much Torah knowledge and mitzvoth as they wished; only, they did not do so. And now their spirit is dry, without sustenance, and they stagnate in their spiritual poverty and distress. As Scripture attests about them, they have no one, nothing to comfort them — since they took no trouble to provide for themselves spiritually while there was still time.

16
ONLY FOR THE "CASH" OF THE TORAH'S LIGHT

If we want to attain life in the ultimate future, to return to life at the resurrection, we have to learn a great deal of Torah. For without the radiance of the Torah, a man's other merits and virtues will not be enough to enable him to rise up alive at the revival of the dead.

Let us explain with a parable: A storekeeper once came to a cloth factory to buy various materials for his store (shop). The manager of the factory set before him all the various kinds of cloths made in the factory, and he chose what he needed out of each kind. When all his purchases were neatly wrapped and tied, the man saw that one quantity of material, which he had particularly liked, had been left aside and not packed up with the other goods that he had bought. "Why did you not include this material", he asked the manager, "with the other things that I have purchased? I wrote it down in the list of things I wanted."

"O", said the manager, "that is a very expensive cloth that we make in limited quantity. You won't find anything like it in any other factory around here. So we sell it only for payment in cash. But you are buying on credit."

At the time of the great resurrection, when the longed-for moment arrives at last and the dead awaken to life, those who do not revive will come bearing their merits and virtues in hand, demanding the right also to come alive, so that they can bask in the radiance of the seven days after the resurrection. All will be told, however, that only an individual who possesses the illumination of Torah will be worthy enough to rise from his tomb to eternal life, whereas other merits and virtues are not sufficient to bring a person back to the living.

Thus Scripture says, *For Thy dew is the dew of light* (Isaiah 26:19);

and the Sages comment: Whoever possesses the light of Torah, the Torah's light will bring him alive; and whoever does not possess the light of Torah, the Torah's light will not revive him.

17
IT IS NOT THEIRS

There are people who are ready to compromise on everything regarding the Torah and the observance of its mitzvoth. They are perfectly willing to give way about this, to overlook that, as long as they do not get into any conflict with non-religious people. They will make any concession, just to keep those people quiet.

They can be compared to a man who was once seen taking precious, expensive goods out of a shop, whereupon he ran with them to the river and threw them in. The people who saw him doing this bizarre thing decided that the poor man must have gone out of his mind. Which sensible person would ever do a thing like that?

"And yet", said the Ḥafetz Ḥayyim, "I myself am yet in doubt if that man was really deranged or not. Of one thing I am certain, though, past any doubt: The shop from which the man took out the things was not his own; and the merchandise he threw into the river was not his own.

"And the same is true of those people who are ready to compromise and make concessions, accepting all kinds of various 'reforms' in the Torah and the observance of its mitzvoth. They are like the man who ran to the river to throw in the expensive merchandise. By being so ready to give way and reach an understanding at the expense of our holy Torah and its mitzvoth they make it very plain that the 'shop' is not theirs, and the 'merchandise' is not theirs. For if those people felt that the Torah was really theirs, the source of their life-energy and the matrix of their existence, they would certainly never yield, no matter what, even over some minor sacred custom of our forefathers."

18
NOW ANY MERCHANDISE IS ACCEPTABLE

For our numerous sins, in our time the spiritual life of our people is at a very low level, indeed in a sorry state. Yet because of this, strange as it may sound, everyone in Jewry can now do a thriving "business" with the blessed Lord, if we may so speak.

If this seems hard to understand, said the Ḥafetz Ḥayyim, it can be explained with a story:

A very wealthy Jew who carried on a large trade in grains, made his home in one of the large cities in Russia, but he conducted his business far and wide, in all parts of the country. When the First World War broke out, in 1914, he came to the Ḥafetz Ḥayyim to bemoan his fate in those distressing, agonizing times, insisting that he saw no satisfying results from his business activities. Even though his trade in the country had grown tremendously, and he now kept sending large shipments of grain, sometimes even taking whole carloads of wheat himself to the flour mill, the market was flooded with produce, and the tradesmen themselves were forcing the price down. Apart from this, it was necessary to sell on long-term credit, allowing large periods of time for payments. In short, he was doing a large amount of business, but making very little profit.

A few years later the Soviet revolution broke out, bringing in its wake a great famine through the entire land of Russia. Once again the merchant came to see the Ḥafetz Ḥayyim. Now, however, as if by a miracle, his face was elated, and he looked in general like a man who had had a stroke of good fortune. "Well", said the Ḥafetz Ḥayyim, "how are you? And how is your business faring?"

"Heaven be thanked", said the man. "Now I am making good profits."

"How is that?" the Ḥafetz Ḥayyim wondered. "We have a famine in the land. There is a severe food shortage; no wheat at all is to be found; all the granaries are empty; the flour mills are idled ... and you say that fortune is smiling on your business activities? How could that be?"

"That is the very reason", said the merchant. "Previously, when the times were in order, the bakers insisted on high-grade flour, and so the mills insisted on fine, superior wheat, of select grade. Whatever grain I brought them they examined seven times, and they would turn up their noses and reject my merchandise time and again. Around every buyer there were twenty merchants hanging about trying to sell. So business was very bad — really in the dumps.

"Today there is a serious famine in the land. You can hardly find any wheat for sale anywhere. When I come to a dealer with a bit of grain to sell, he almost grabs it out of my hand, you might say. He pays me any price I ask. And he is not even interested in examining the quality. So of course I am now making very handsome profits."

Well (the Ḥafetz Ḥayyim would draw the moral of the story) if that is how things go in the grain and flour business, surely it must be even more true for Torah and mitzvoth! In olden times there were people with great minds, and the academies and houses of study were filled to the brim with students. The "Torah market" was flooded only with "high quality merchandise": Torah for its own sake, studied in holiness and purity; good deeds done with the benevolent intention of the heart. If someone came and brought "merchandise" into the "market" that was not of the highest quality, even if it had the slightest defect — alien thoughts during one's prayer, Torah study not for its own sake but for ulterior motives, a mitzvah done without the good intent and focus of the heart but absent-mindedly — no one wanted merchandise like that.

Now, for our many sins, the Torah academies are empty of students. The houses of study remain abandoned, without a soul in them. The students and scholars have wandered off. Even plain Jews who only keep up daily prayer with a congregation, are dwindling in number. It is a time of crisis, truly a period of drought and famine. Now, any "merchandise" brought into the "market" is snatched up, be it even Torah study not for its own intrinsic sake, even if not in purity and holiness — as long as it is some kind of "merchandise". And for everything, top prices are paid, at the same rate that was once paid for the finest quality merchandise.

Let this be borne in mind by all those who are too lazy or reluctant to study Torah, arguing that their minds are not clear and fit for this learning, that they cannot properly focus their heart and concentrate. Now is the very best time for this "business activity".

19
WHY THE TORAH SUIT DOES NOT FIT

A tailor once sewed a suit to order for a customer. The man came and took it home, but in a few days he was back, full of complaints: The suit did not fit properly. It was too big for him, and when he wore it, it seemed to be hanging on him every which way.

The tailor told him to put it on, and he examined it carefully. Then he chuckled. "I will tell you what the trouble is", he said. "I am not at fault, and the suit is not at fault. When I measured you and sewed it up, it would have fit you fine. But during this time you have gone and lost considerable weight, while the suit remained the same size."

For our many sins, we see countless people today who have drawn far away from the Torah and such basic religious practices as wearing t'fillin (phylacteries) and tzitzith (ritual tassels at the corners of a four-cornered garment, to keep a person reminded of the mitzvoth). We might think mistakenly that they have risen so high in intelligence and understanding that the Torah and t'fillin are no longer suitable for them. They are perhaps above all that.

Well, it is not so at all, but just the opposite: The heads of these people have (spiritually) shrunk, until an ordinary pair of t'fillin can no longer fit so small a head. The Torah, that encompasses the whole world in its lessons of truth, can no longer fit into so small and shrunken a brain. So the t'fillin falls from their head, and the Torah draws far away from them to become totally alien.

Thus Scripture says, *it is no empty thing for you* (Deuteronomy 32:47), and the Sages comment: If you find the Torah empty, it is empty *for you* — on account of the emptiness in you!

20
THE RAILWAY OF RELIGIOUS LAW

The Ḥafetz Ḥayyim invested a tremendous amount of work in his *Mishnah B'rurah,* his unparalleled commentary on *Shulḥan Aruch Oraḥ Ḥayyim.* Days and nights he labored and toiled over every paragraph. Great as his faith was in Jewry's sages and scholars, when he found authorities quoted in earlier works on religious law, he did not rely on the quotations but checked everything in original sources. With application and precision he went carefully over every view and opinion in the law, starting from a discussion in the Talmud and following it through to the most recent authority in religious law.

For some part of the great task, his son R. Leyb (of blessed memory) was able to help him. Once, as the two sat working together, his son remarked, "I doubt very much if those who study this work will ever know how much toil and labor and immense effort has gone into every little paragraph and subsection."

"Let me give you a parable about it, my son", said the Ḥafetz Ḥayyim. And this is what he told:

You must surely have seen how they put the steel rails in place for the railway line. Many hundreds of laborers work away at it for a year or more. It is hard, backbreaking work. Yet if time runs short and they must meet a pressing schedule, they will work at night too, even in the cold and the rain, until they have set dozens of miles of steel rails.

Once a man came along and saw the laborers toiling away at their harsh task for a very long time. He could not understand it. "Why do you have to do all that backbreaking work?" he asked. "What do you need all that bitter toil for? Why is so much money being sunk into this project?"

"Your eyes see well enough what is going on", the foreman answered him in scorn, "but your mind doesn't grasp the purpose of it all. When this big project is finished, there will be a line of steel rails linking up the main cities of the land. The railroad trains will then travel on them at great speed, carrying hundreds of passengers. The people will be able to travel in comfort, protected from rain, storm and cold. A person will save days when he has to travel. Then, when the railway system is operating smoothly, you will be able to appreciate how worthwhile it was to put in all this hard, heavy work at such great cost — just to prepare the way for the railroad."

It is the same with us (the Ḥafetz Ḥayyim concluded). True, we are investing a great amount of energy and effort in this work. We are laboring night and day and can barely manage to reach our desired goal in time. Yet eventually, with the blessed Lord's help, we will be privileged to thank Him for seeing it done. Then the Jewish people will be able to learn the *Shulḥan Aruch* (the code of religious law) with a new will and eagerness, along the new, clear and easy path that we shall have paved for them; and they will reach their destination easily — a thorough knowledge of every single law, without any doubt or uncertainty. The study of the laws will thus spread through Jewry, to the greater glory and honor of our blessed Lord. To reach that goal, it is worth investing all this immense effort and energy, even if some will never know how hard we have had to toil to make this paved road.

21
STANDING FIRM AT THE MILITARY POST

An emperor once sent word to one of his army generals that on this-and-this day he had to be ready and prepared for a royal visit of inspection, since he (the emperor) intended to come that day and inspect the troops.

When the day came, all was ready, spick and span, in that general's ranks. Every soldier was in his clean, neatly pressed uniform, hair brushed, shoes sparkling; and they stood in their ranks with military precision. At their head stood the general himself, adorned in military dress, waiting at attention for his emperor's arrival.

When would the emperor come, though? He had written that he would arrive at nine. Yet here it was well past the hour, and there was still no sign of him. Every few minutes the general glanced at his watch, looked out toward the entrance of the army camp, and frowned. A half hour went by, and still the emperor had not come. Under the morning sun the troops stood in their perfect ranks, and waited in utter silence. An hour went by, then two hours, and three . . . and there was yet no sign of the emperor. Where was he? When was he coming? No one knew. . . .

At last, tired of standing with all his men under the hot sun, the general decided to take a rest. If he stood there any longer at attention, he felt he would go out of his mind. He called over an ordinary soldier to take his place, and he himself went off to some quiet shady corner to rest his weary feet. As soon as he caught sight of the emperor, the soldier was to come at once to call him back.

The soldier, however, was not too alert either, and the sudden appearance of the emperor caught him unawares. There was no time to warn the general. Before that poor officer realized what was happening and scrambled back to his place at the head of his troops, it was too late for him to give the emperor his official military welcome.

The emperor realized only too well what had occurred here, and he was furious with the general. From that officer's uniform he ripped off the stars of his high rank, and he dismissed him from his post. The man was banished from the military service. In his place, the emperor appointed the soldier who had stood guard for the general.

As the demoted general stood there, crestfallen and humiliated, the emperor berated him soundly: "You were the general of this entire army division. You held a high, distinguished rank. You received handsome pay from the royal treasury. On the other hand, here is a plain soldier, an ordinary private. No one recognizes him especially. I do not even know his name. And the pay he receives from the royal treasury is quite small. Nevertheless he stood here faithfully at his post, patiently waiting for my arrival. He did not give way to weariness and fatigue, and he did not abandon his post. And you, a distinguished senior officer, left your troops and went off to rest!"

This is how it will be in the ultimate future. We all keep waiting in expectation for our righteous redeemer, the royal Messiah. Then we have to be ready to receive him properly, in repentance for our sins and with good deeds to our credit. With these we have to hold firm and stand faithfully at our posts, expectant and prepared for his arrival. Without these, though, how can we possibly hold firm and really await him? And if (Heaven forbid) we abandon our place in the ranks and do not stand strong to receive him when he comes, how can we hold up our heads? How can we look up to our Father in heaven if we leave our ranks broken, with gaping holes, when the royal Messiah will suddenly appear before us?

We observant Jews who live by the Torah are the generals in the Almighty's army of the spirit, the senior officers in the ranks of the supreme King of kings, the Holy Blessed One. We must certainly stand ready at our posts, with Torah study and prayer and good deeds, all prepared to welcome the royal Messiah, the righteous redeemer, when he comes — may it be speedily in our day.

22
RAIN AND DEW

Rain and dew both bring moisture to the soil; but there is a difference between them: Rain falls in single drops, whereas dew condenses and lies spread over the ground all at once. Hence the rainfall in a particular location can be measured, while the dewdrops cannot, since they appear all at once.

This is the nature of the difference between the Written and the Oral Torah.

The Written Torah contains the 613 mitzvoth (precepts, commandments), while the Oral Torah explains and clarifies the Written one. When Moses our master wished to adjure the Israelites in his Divinely inspired song to keep the Torah and its mitzvoth faithfully, down to the last detail, he said, *Let my teaching drop as the rain, let my speech distill as the dew* (Deuteronomy 32:2). He meant: The Written Torah, the timeless teaching of the Holy Blessed One to the Jewish people, is in the nature of rain — because the mitzvoth of the Torah can be counted: there are 613 of them. On the other hand, the Oral Torah is in the nature of dew, because the teachings of the Talmud are wider than the ocean, and cannot be counted or measured.

23
THE THREE CHARACTERISTICS

Gifts can be divided into three categories: (1) if the gift by itself is not of great value, but by contrast the one who gives it is a man of great worth or eminence, such as a king or one of the important government ministers. When a person like that gives a present, the giving of it is of more significance than the present itself. (2) when the person giving it is not distinguished, and there is no pride to be taken in receiving it from *him,* but the present itself is of considerable value. (3) a present whose value grows with time, because it is something rare and very difficult to find.

Our sacred Torah excels in all three characteristics together. This is why the Holy Blessed One tells the Jewish people, *I have given you good instruction* (Proverbs 4:2) — the Torah is itself a precious, valuable gift, worth more than all the wealth in the world. Moreover, it is "I", the supreme King of kings, the Holy Blessed One, who gives you this present. Then its value to us is greater a thousand times over. Beyond that, it is more precious than pearls, since it can be attained by none but select, chosen gifted individuals.

Then *do not abandon My Torah* (*ibid.*): Guard this precious possession like the apple of your eye.

24
TO OWN A HOME FOR THE SPIRIT

How does a man get to own a house? He can go to a store that sells building materials and buy everything he needs to build a house: bricks, timber, cement, and so forth. Then he can go and dig the foundations, pour the concrete, and work and toil through every task, putting the timbers and beams in place, setting the bricks, slaving away until by the sweat of his brow the house is all constructed and standing in place.

Another man, however, may be blessed from heaven to gather enough money to buy a house. He may go and purchase one that is already built and standing, which he can afford; or he may get an architect's plan and hire construction workers, and they will build it for him.

There is no real difference among these kinds: They are all homeowners.

Well, the same is true about the Torah. On the verse, *Wisdom has built her house* (Proverbs 9:1) the Sages comment in Midrash Mishley that "it means the Torah: Whoever acquires words of Torah for himself acquires a house for himself in the world-to-come (the Hereafter)". In their hallowed phrasing, the Sages were precise: they did not state, "Whoever learns Torah", but "Whoever acquires Torah", and the Hebrew for "acquires", *kanah,* also denotes purchasing — to teach us that not only a person who studies the Torah thus builds himself a home in the world-to-come, but also a man who supports Torah study with his money. He too builds himself a home there, by maintaining the places and students engaged in this sacred study. And there is no real difference between a home bought or built.

25
AT FIRST TO BE REVIVED

Some people traveling on the road looked out and saw a man lying by the wayside, bleeding profusely. They stopped their vehicle at once and leaped out, to try to help him. One examined his wounds and looked for ways to stop the bleeding. Another looked in his belongings for clean bandages, and he set to work to bandage the wounds. A third tried to move him gently, so that he could examine him and see if there were any more serious wounds, of which they did not know. They worked thus for a while, each at his task — yet the injured man remained unconscious, showing hardly any signs of life.

As they kept working away, a doctor happened along. He stopped to come over and examine the man, paying little attention to what the three were doing to help the wounded person. Then he spoke: "You had better stop all that now. As you can see, the man is deeply unconscious and only barely alive. I must first give him a medicine to restore his vitality and return him to consciousness. Only after he returns to his senses can we deal with his wounds."

Our Sages said: Even all the mitzvoth (commandments) of the Torah are not to be compared to one word of the Torah (Jerusalem Talmud, Pé'ah i). Whatever does it mean? — The mitzvoth are, in truth, a healing for a man; they strengthen and uphold him on his feet all his life. This is all well and good, however, only when he needs nothing more than strengthening and healing. A man who has no Torah learning, though, can only be regarded as unconscious, in a coma, and his spiritual·life is in danger. He must therefore learn Torah first of all, to restore his spiritual vitality. Afterward the mitzvoth can maintain a person in good spiritual health.

For this reason, all the mitzvoth together cannot compare to one word of Torah. One sacred word of it can revive a man and instill a new life-spirit in him.

26
CLEAN, OR TATTERED AND STAINED?

Did you ever see a young boy's textbook for his holy studies — a volume of the Talmud or the Hebrew Bible? Did you ever see how it looks? — It is all stained and spotted with pen and pencil marks. Scribbles and doodles "adorn" every page. The margins are occasionally torn, and it is altogether wrinkled and tattered. You can hardly recognize it as a holy volume.

On the other hand, when an adult studies a printed volume of Torah learning, he is generally careful about the appearance of the work and makes sure to keep it clean, knowing it is holy and must be kept free of any stain, and nothing but notes on the Torah study may be written on its pages.

Now come, let us make a reckoning: Let us see how we do our studying of the Torah. When we sit down to learn our daily lesson at its set time, we generally interrupt from time to time with talk of no consequence. We do not even hesitate to relate matters of evil gossip and slander during our learning period. And sometimes, between one line of Torah and another, we may even be full of laughter, convulsed by some fine joke.

After this life on earth has ended we will stand before the heavenly court of justice, and we will be asked: "Did you engage in the study of Torah?" *O yes,* we will reply confidently. There and then the angels will bring all the volumes we studied — and we will be mortally ashamed to see how the volumes of Hebrew Bible and Talmud and other holy works are all torn and tattered with our many interruptions, and deeply stained and scribbled by our evil gossip, slander, and pointless idle chit-chat.

How careful we must then be during our periods of sacred study, not to interrupt with anything that is unconnected with the Torah.

27
WHOLESALE IS BETTER

A fine young man with a good Talmudic education was very active on behalf of the yeshivah (Torah academy) in Slutsk, Lithuania. He was able to prevail on wealthy Jews to support it, and persuaded good, promising students to attend it and improve their learning. . . . In the course of time, though, a nearby town needed a new rabbi (the old one having died), and since he was a very learned young man, the position was offered him.

The young man was of two minds: Should he give up his work for the yeshivah and take the rabbinic position? Or was it better to forgo the rabbinate for the sake of his efforts on behalf of the yeshivah, because that was more important? Unable to decide, he went to ask the Ḥafetz Ḥayyim what to do.

"You see", said the young man, "if I take the position of rabbi, I will have more free time to sit and study Torah. Now I have little time for it."

The Ḥafetz Ḥayyim nodded in understanding. "Tell me something, though", he asked. "When a shoemaker sews a pair of shoes to order, how much does he charge?"

"Oh, about five rubles."

"And how much does a pair of shoes from the factory cost?"

"Oh, perhaps two rubles."

"Now", said the Ḥafetz Ḥayyim, "how much profit do you think the shoemaker earns out of the five rubles?"

"I would say a ruble and a half."

"And how much does the factory net from a pair of shoes?"

"Only twenty or thirty cents."

"Well then", said the Ḥafetz Ḥayyim, "is it not amazing that the shoemaker is a rather poor man, barely making a living with difficulty, while the owner of the factory, who makes such a very small profit on a pair of shoes, is extremely wealthy?"

The answer was easy, the young man explained. True, the shoe-maker earned more from a pair of his shoes, but he was unable to turn out more than two or three pairs a week. The factory, on the other hand, employing hundreds of workers, was able to produce hundreds of pairs every day. That was why the owner earned vastly more than the shoemaker, although he took a far smaller price.

"Well then", said the Ḥafetz Ḥayyim, "I think that answers your question. Quite certainly, when you will serve as rabbi in that town, you will have more time to study Torah during the day. Yet what a vast difference there is between your sacred study as an individual, by yourself, and the focused learning of hundreds of students at the yeshivah, every one of whom studies for ten hours or more during the day and continues on through part of the night. Even if you get in your heavenly account only a small percent of the merit for that Torah study of hundreds of pupils, your reward is very great."

28
THE MANSION BEYOND THE ENTRANCE-HALL

When a wealthy man buys or builds a home, it is generally very spacious, containing many rooms and chambers, each serving a different purpose. Past the door there is the entrance hall or reception room, where people can leave their coats and hats, overshoes and galoshes, etc. Such a room or hall is generally furnished sparsely and simply, as it is only the place of entry.

The second room will generally be furnished better, since it is used at times to receive visitors for brief conversation, before they are taken to the main visitors' room.

The third room is usually the study, used by the wealthy head of the family for his work. Here new, expensive furniture is to be found: a large handsome desk with ornate pens, and so forth; a beautiful carpet covering the floor; heavily upholstered leather chairs; a splendid filing cabinet, perhaps.... The fourth room might be the large hall or chamber for receiving visitors, splendidly furnished in palatial style, with inviting sofas and easy chairs, a refectory table with handsome crystal-ware; beautiful ashtrays and bowls of fruit; and so on.

Then of course there are bedrooms for all the members of the family, and perhaps a number of guest-rooms, for visitors who stay a while. Leading off from the master bedroom there may be a small private chamber, kept under lock and key, where the owner keeps his most valuable documents, a supply of cash, and his wife's costly jewelry.

This world of ours, though, is only an entrance-hall to the world-to-come. So it is sparsely and simply furnished, with plain pieces of furniture — just enough for the daily needs of the people passing through. In the ultimate future, however, when the righteous Messiah comes and knowledge of the Lord will cover the earth as water covers the sea, then all the immense treasures that lie concealed in the holy Torah and its mitzvoth will be revealed. Then the blessed Lord will show us the spiritual palatial mansion, room after room, where every honor and glory has been kept to be bestowed on the scholars who have studied and worked to spread a knowledge of the Torah.

Today they are but poorly esteemed and little honored. In the entrance-hall that makes up our world there are no expensive furnishings and rich accommodations for the outstanding Torah scholars of the generation, by whose merit the world endures. Only in the ultimate future of the Messianic era will all see what lies ahead for them beyond the entrance-hall.

29
INFERIOR AND SUPERIOR WEAPONS

Among all the royal servants who worked for a king in his palace, there was one particular servant who was outstanding in his devotion to the sovereign ruler. He bore the king a strong affection, and was ready to do anything for him.

The time came when the king had to go to war, to repulse an invading enemy. He summoned his troops and began distributing weapons and ammunition to them, so that they could set off for battle. As he paused in his task, his devoted palace servant came up. In his strong affection for the king, he insisted on going along and fighting in the ranks. "But, your majesty", he said, "I ask your permission to prepare my own weapons, at my own expense. It will be my privilege." The king granted his permission, and the servant went off happily to make his preparations.

His enthusiasm, though, was stronger than the arms and armor that he was able to prepare. In the heat of battle, while he was fighting in the front lines, he found that his weapons broke and spoiled, and could no longer be used. In great haste he ran to the king and asked if he might have some of the standard army equipment. The king simply laughed at him: "What a fool you are! Why do you have to ask permission for that? We are all battling for our lives here. Take any weapons and ammunition you find, as long as you can help us win!"

What is the moral of the story? Our "king" is the Almighty, and we are His devoted servants, whom He treats as His children and loyal friends. Here on this earth we find ourselves in a constant hard battle against the evil (satanic) inclination, that seeks to incite us to rebellion against our Divine Sovereign. Our weapons and ammunition are the holy Torah we learn and the mitzvoth we keep.

There are some persons, though, who privately believe that since they have been worthy to have their sons studying Torah, they have already fulfilled their obligation to take up arms and join in the battle. Their sons, they feel, are their own special "armament, prepared by themselves at their own expense". They feel no obligation to study Torah themselves and support yeshivoth (Torah academies) and Torah scholars generally.

Alas, they make a great error. In this difficult battle we have to use every kind of weapon and ammunition that we can get. And supporting the study of Torah is the very best weaponry in this conflict. By learning Torah ourselves and supporting its students and scholars, we can attain a decisive victory over the evil inclination.

II: MITZVOTH

30

THE HATEFUL FRIENDLY TALK

A Jew once went hurry-scurrying through the street, coattails flying, hat set atilt on his head. He had no time to lose. Every moment was precious to him, as he ran about attending to his affairs. Who could take it as a laughing matter? He was doing his best to earn a living, having a wife and children to support, a household of hungry mouths to feed.

As he ran along, an acquaintance of his stopped him. "You fool", he asked, "where are you running like that? Why do you tire yourself out like that all day? Whatever you do, you are not going to become as rich as Rothschild. Then why all the hustle and bustle? You would do better to stay home and rest."

The first man just stared at his acquaintance in amazement: "It seems to me, my good man, if you will forgive my saying so, that *you* are talking like a fool. Just because I can never be as rich as Rothschild, I should sit at home with folded hands? If I stop working altogether, there won't even be a crust of dry bread in my house!"

Often the satanic evil inclination comes to a man with a beguiling argument: "Is it at all worthwhile for you to put in so much toil and wearying effort in order to do a mitzvah (a religious good deed)? Of course, if it happens to come your way and you have a chance to observe it without any toil or trouble, go ahead and do it. But if you see that it is no easy matter, get well out of the whole thing and forget it!"

Know therefore what answer to give that vile satanic scoundrel: By doing nothing and sitting idle a man will never earn a "living" for his spirit in the world-to-come. Even if we do the easy mitzvoth that come along, that we can observe without effort, the reward for them is not very great.

Above all, we have to remember that this satanic evil inclination comes as a friend, beguiling and persuasive, pretending to have our interests at heart. Only when the time comes for the final reward, in the Hereafter, does it emerge in its true colors, as not a friend at all but as Satan, our mortal enemy.

It is the same when a person listens to evil gossip. When one man tells another all kinds of slanderous news and evil gossip, the listener's heart is moved by feelings of affection for the one talking to him, because it is so pleasant to hear such things. He feels sure that the person speaking to him must be a true friend and companion, since the man is revealing secret matters to him.

In the Afterlife, however, we will find ourselves in a world of truth. There, when the time comes to receive our just reward for all our actions on earth, the one who has listened to the slanderous talk and the evil gossip must pay for the pleasure he had at the time. Then he realizes what a price he must pay for that "true friendship" and "affection" that he felt for the other person, and it turns into bitter hatred.

31
UNDESERVED PAYMENT

We read in Scripture, *to Thee, O Lord, belongs loving-kindness, for Thou dost recompense a man according to his work* (Psalms 62:13). Well, many have wondered and asked: What wonderful news is it that He rewards a man according to his deeds? It is only fair and just for a man to receive his proper due. Then if the Divine Master of the world gives a man his due, what reason is that to praise and extol him?

It can be explained, though, with a parable: A youngster was once hired out as an apprentice to a craftsman, so that he could learn the man's skill. It was agreed between them that the lad had to work for the craftsman for five years. All his needs — food, clothing, and so on — had to be provided by his employer. And in the fifth year, when the lad would already know how to do his work properly, the craftsman was to pay him forty dollars a week.

The years went by, and the youngster learned the craft. In the fifth year, true to his word, his employer began paying him forty dollars a week. The youngster learned, however, that others who worked in the shop were paid far more: Some received 250 dollars a week, and some 300. Once he knew that, he came to his employer to complain, "How can you treat me like that? I am doing good work now, just as fine and skilled as what those workers produce. Then why do I get only forty dollars a week when they get so much more?"

"You", said the craftsman, "are nothing but a fool. How can you come and compare yourself to those men? Did I ever have to sweat and toil to teach them the craft? They were skilled experienced workers when they came here. They did not spoil my tools and equipment while they were learning the vocation. Even now they do not use my tools but their own. The food and clothing they need never costs me a penny. So I have to pay them a full salary. You, on the other hand, have learned your trade here. You spoiled and broke my work tools while you were learning what to do. And I have to maintain you with meals and clothing. Right now, even the forty dollars I give you is more than you deserve."

This will give us an idea of what Scripture means. Whenever we do a mitzvah, we do it with the tools and equipment of the Holy Blessed One. Where did we get the arm on which we put the t'fillin of the hand? — it is His creation. The mouth a man uses to chant His praises, was given us by Him. He sustains us and provides for us, giving us all we lack. All we have comes from Him.

Then how much of a salary or payment can we deserve for our mitzvoth that we do? — surely not very much. Nevertheless, the Almighty "recompenses a man according to his work": He rewards him *in full* for his mitzvoth and good deeds.

32
NO PAYMENT TOO SMALL

There was once a very wealthy man who was also greatly learned and wise. The time came, however, when the tide of fortune turned against him, and he lost all his money. He had no choice but to go and look for work. Too embarrassed, though, to take a job far beneath his former dignity and prestige in his own town, he went to far-off locations where no one knew him; and there he made the rounds, trudging from one factory or shop to another, looking for any employment that would let him earn enough to keep body and soul together.

Of course, wherever he went he was asked, "How much do you want?"

"Three hundred dollars a week."

The answer to that was always, "We are sorry". No one had any need for such a high-salaried employee. Doggedly he kept traveling here and there, always looking and searching. Thus weeks went by, until he had barely a penny left in his pocket, out of the little bit of money that he had managed to salvage from his former wealth. As he trudged on, he now suffered the pangs of hunger. He had no choice left but to take work at whatever salary he could get — a hundred dollars a week.

Some time later he happened to meet an old acquaintance. They greeted each other warmly and took to talking. The first man told his unhappy story, how he had lost his money and come down in the world, until he now had to work for a hundred dollars a week.

"How could that be?" the other wondered. "You are so wise and learned; you have abilities. How can a man like you work for such a small salary?"

"What could I do?" the first man replied. "I had to keep body and soul together. It came to the point where I was literally suffering from hunger. Do you think I had any choice? I had to take even work like this. It is better to earn even a hundred dollars a week than to walk the streets idle."

We would do well to learn to think the same way and make the same kind of calculation in this lowly world, when it comes to doing mitzvoth. We really cannot afford to be choosy and spurn some mitzvoth as not worth the trouble. Perish the thought that we should let any opportunity for a mitvah go by. Whatever we can do or observe, let us hasten and do it. However large or small the reward for it may be, in the Hereafter we will desperately need every bit of spiritual payment that we have earned on this earth.

33
TWO SISTERS, TWO ATTITUDES

There were once two sisters who married and went to live in two towns that were quite far from one another. As fate decreed, one found herself wealthy, and the other poor. Because of the great distance between them, they could see each other only once every few years; and then they would tell each other everything that had happened to them since the last time they had met.

Once the poor sister came to visit the wealthy one and stay with her a while; and she was stunned to see how her well-to-do sister looked. "Tell me," she said, "why do you look so poorly and run-down? You are so prosperous, you lack for nothing, and everyone in the family is (thank Heaven) alive and well. You have no worries at all about meeting expenses. Then why do you look so wan and gaunt? Why have you become so thin?"

The wealthy sister opened her heart and poured out her bitter story, to reveal the tragedy of her life. At first the poor sister could hardly believe her ears; but the other one assured her that it was true: In all her life of wealth and affluence, she found not one moment of goodness and satisfaction. She had never known happiness. "What is the good of all the wealth?" she wept. "What does it help me to have all this plenty, if I can find no pleasure at all in my family? You are my sister, my own flesh-and-blood. To you I can tell the plain bitter truth. The source of all my trouble is my husband. He makes my life a torment, literally a hell. He treats me so atrociously, without any respect for me, so that even the servant-girl doesn't respect me; and he thinks more of her than he thinks of me. Whatever I say he contradicts, as if deliberately to get me angry; or he pays no attention to what I say. Before strangers he treats me with respect; but in the house, when we are alone, he degrades and humiliates me like some fishwife. Is it any wonder then that I look like this?

"At times I cannot even understand how I can go on living in such torment; how I have not gone down to an early grave. . . . So you see, my dear sister: You have a hard life running your family, you have trouble making ends meet, and your health is not altogether in order either. You have never known the feeling of having enough money. And yet your face looks as good as if you had been living in the lap of luxury, as if you had been wealthier and happier than myself."

"Well," said her poorer sister, "you are right about that. I still have a cheerful, good-looking face; but it is only thanks to my husband. God be thanked and praised, that man of mine does anything I ask him, and he always likes to please me. The life-partner that the good Lord gave me has a sweeter disposition than I do. He always asks my opinion before he does anything. He won't make a move without me. And that sweetens my life until I don't feel the poverty and hardship at all. My husband's love is worth more to me than all the wealth in the world."

Well, the story of these two sisters is the story of the attitudes that people take toward the mitzvoth of our holy Torah.

There are people who show a great deal of respect for the Torah, paying it honor and tribute — outwardly. They are willing to pay handsomely to be called to the reading of the Torah at important occasions. They will donate money for fixtures or decorations in the synagogue, in memory of departed parents. They will provide expensive velvet hangings for the holy ark, and velvet coverings for Torah scrolls. Alone, however, in the innermost room of their home, they will freely violate all the mitzvoth, treating the Torah like a doormat. They will desecrate the Sabbath, eat non-kosher food, and thus treat with contempt other matters that are absolute fundamentals of our Torah.

In contrast to them, there are poor simple persons who do not have the means to honor the Torah with money. Instead, though, they honor it in private, in every way that they can. They will avoid doing anything bad. They make the Sabbath a delight by refraining from attending to any business on that day. They scrupulously avoid theft and robbery and any kind of dishonesty.

Now, consider: The Torah is perceived metaphorically as the beautiful bride given to our people at Mount Sinai. Is she then not far happier with a poor man who respects and honors her with all his heart, than with a man of means who squanders money on her freely but in his heart is not in harmony with her?

34

THE GEMS BY THE ROADSIDE

A certain poor, penniless Jew was blessed with a family of many children, but alas, had no way of providing for them properly. All his days he struggled against hardships and handicaps in an effort to find work so that he could support himself and his family; but he never succeeded in earning even barely enough.

One day he was walking along the road in bitter despair, since he knew that in the house there was not even food enough for one meal, and there was no prospect in sight of earning any money. As he walked on with his head lowered, something flashed across his vision. He turned his head, and saw a brilliant colored object lying at the road-side — perhaps a piece of broken glass. It was quite certainly nothing to bother about, he thought. It was probably best to keep walking and not waste time over it. Still, he decided, it couldn't hurt to stop and have a look at it. Maybe it had some small value, and he could use it to buy a piece of bread for his children.

He stooped down and picked it up — and could hardly believe his eyes. It was a sparkling polished jewel set in precious metal, that flashed, glinted and blazed in all the colors of the rainbow as he turned it in his hand. He was on a main road between two towns. Whoever lost it had been traveling and was not likely to be back looking for it, not even knowing where he had lost it. But what sort of precious stone was it? And how much was it worth?

As fast as his legs could carry him, he made for a jeweler in his town. The jeweler examined the stone under his enlarging-glass, and whistled in amazement. "I have never seen a gem like this", he said. "It belongs in the crown of the king. I shall write the royal palace about it, and we will see what happens."

In a short while the king's messengers came to take the poor man and his jewel to the palace. There the king and his advisors examined the stone, and they too were greatly impressed. They found it so beautiful and flawless that they could hardly stop praising it. At last the king called the poor man to him.

"Well, my good fellow", he said, "how much do you want for it?"

The man shrugged his shoulders. "Your majesty, how could I possibly know what price to ask? Until I brought it to the jeweler I did not even know it was valuable."

"Very well", said the king; and at his order the poor man went home a rich man, the owner of a small fortune.

What is the moral of the story? Observant Jews learn the Torah and keep the mitzvoth, with no idea at all of what their value is. Wherever they are, walking along the road of life, when they find a bright, shining mitzvah to be done, they pick up the opportunity and do it eagerly. They know that Divine reward is promised for keeping the mitzvoth — reward more precious than fine gold and jewels. Yet this is not what they have in mind, because mitzvoth have to be observed for their own sake. They are commanded to pick up every such precious gem that they find by the road of life, without ever really knowing how much or little it may be worth, how much recompense will be awaiting them in the Afterlife.

They know however, that the Divine Sovereign, the supreme King of kings, can be trusted implicitly. He will pay each and every one faithfully for every precious gem of a mitzvah that he has observed in his journey through life.

35
THE MISTREATED MERCHANDISE

When a shopkeeper has merchandise to sell, and especially if it is really goods of high quality, he will never stop recommending and praising it, listing all its good features, one by one. Even if the wares are not really of such fine quality, the shopkeeper will do all he can to make them look as good and attractive as he can, and he will still praise them to his customers. He will clean and polish the merchandise and set it out attractively, so that it will make a good impression on a customer. For example, if a man has a diamond which is not of the very best quality, he will do his best to polish and set it in such a way that a person examining it should hardly notice its flaws.

Suppose, then, that one particular tradesman, as a matter of policy, would never do anything to enhance and improve his wares, at least in appearance, to make customers eager to buy them, but on the contrary he would deliberately let everything in his store look bad, spoiled or damaged. Fellow-tradesmen would have the greatest scorn for him, even wondering if he was in his right mind. Hardly ever would he find a customer willing to buy anything from him. And even if someone wished to make a purchase, what sort of price could he ask when all his wares look damaged or second-hand?

And yet it is in the very manner of this imaginary shopkeeper, who is obviously not quite right in the head, that so many people treat their spiritual merchandise: the Torah and the mitzvoth. Inherently, this is excellent, first-rate merchandise, worth more than the finest gold. In the Hereafter, the timeless world of truth, it is paid for at prime rate. Yet what do we find? There are people who make no effort at all to perform a mitzvah properly, with fervor and love, down to the last detail, as we are commanded. They simply perform it any which way, in passing, indifferently, just to be quit of their obligation.

Most certainly a mitzvah will make an entirely different impression if it is done with focused meaning and proper intention, in service to the Holy Blessed One; if it is performed with fervor and care, so that His blessed name is sanctified through it. It will look entirely different from a mitzvah done as a matter of course, just to fulfill an obligation and no more.

It can only mean that such people do not regard the faithful performance of the mitzvoth as a "well-paying business". Otherwise they could never behave in this self-defeating way. They simply do not realize what a serious mistake they are making, since they thus deprive themselves of immense good reward.

36
THE CONDITION OF THE ACCOUNT BOOK

In a certain city there was a wealthy man who developed a strong desire to have a large, fine collection of volumes of Torah learning. He wanted a good private library in his home, the walls to be covered by shelves lined with the great works of Talmudic scholarship, in handsome bindings. He took to buying hundreds and thousands of printed works, old and new, and even rare old editions. Above all, he loved to find special, unusual editions and printings that were extremely rare. It was his goal to become known in the world of Torah learning and bibliography as the owner of a splendid and most valuable private library.

One day he learned that in another city a certain man of wealth had come down in the world. The tide of fortune had turned against him, and that rich man was now forced to sell *his* private library, a large valuable collection of Torah learning. In great happiness, our first rich man sent off someone at once as his agent, with orders to buy as many volumes out of that library for sale as he could. However, the wealthy man warned his agent, he was to make very sure that any volume he bought was a fine print; that the pages were clean and unstained, and that there should be no pages missing at the beginning or the end — as they often were in very old volumes. In addition, said this wealthy man, he wanted the agent to note carefully how many whole sets of the Talmud and the Mishnah there were, how many prayer-books, and how many Hebrew Bibles with commentaries. He could never have enough of these, if they were good editions.

When the agent arrived at his destination, he saw that the reports had not been exaggerated. He had never seen such a large private collection of Torah volumes in his life. They completely filled the shelves that stretched across the walls of several rooms, from ceiling to floor. When the owner learned whom this agent represented, he began showing him about personally, pointing out the choicest items in his collection: the most rare and valuable old editions; the thousands of prayer-books from Hebrew presses of every period and every community in Europe; hundreds of sets of the Pentateuch with commentaries, the

Talmud and the Mishnah; and a wealth of works on Talmudic law —
truly a treasure.

The agent began examining everything slowly and methodically; and
he soon realized that he would have to reject most of this library. The
very defects against which his employer had warned him were all here:
pages missing at the beginning or at the end; pages torn loose or torn
across, or dirty and stained. Working carefully, he was barely able to
assemble a small handful of items to buy: a few Bibles and prayer-
books, and two or three sets of the Mishnah. He found not even one
complete set of Talmud in good condition.

"Have you any set of the works of R. Isaac Alfasi, or the Jerusalem
Talmud, or the Midrashim?" he asked.

"No", said the owner. Shrugging his shoulders, the agent continued
his work, selecting a few dozen volumes of Talmudic works, and prepared to pay for the small group of sacred books that he had chosen.

"Is that all you are taking?" asked the owner in dismay. "What of
all these thousands of volumes? There is not another private collection
as large as this in all of Poland!"

"That may be true", said the agent; "but it seems to me that these
volumes were not properly cared for, as valued books have to be kept.
I have the impression that many of them simply rolled about on the
floor at some time. There are pages ruined by mold and damp. They
were handled by someone with dirty fingers. And it seems to me that
when someone needed a sheet of paper, perhaps to wrap something
in it, he simply took a volume at random and tore out a page! This
may have been a valuable private library, but that is not how it was
treated. Frankly, I am surprised that I even found these few dozen
volumes in good condition, clean and complete."

"These are our life and the length of our days": we say this in our
prayers about the Torah and its mitzvoth. To them we have to give our
entire mind and heart. They have to be the main content and purpose
of our life: to learn the Torah and keep its mitzvoth faithfully. Every
last letter of the Torah, every last detail of a mitzvah is literally a part
of our life.

What will happen, though, when we come before the great court of justice in the Afterlife, and they will begin examining our actions here on earth — how we studied Torah, how we prayed, how we observed the mitzvoth? As it happened when the agent examined the very large private library that was offered for sale, the angelic agents of the heavenly court will find hardly anything whole, perfect and unstained. Everything will be found torn, trammeled, defiled, and with parts missing. In the midst of Torah study we gave way to sinful thoughts. In the midst of our prayer our minds wandered off to other, deplorable matters. Whole days went by when we studied no Torah at all; the pages for those days are simply missing from the Torah-diary of our life — torn out. So many other pages in the book of our life will be found ruined by indolence, or by pursuit after the empty nonsense of this world. . . . And when we shall see, standing before Heaven's court of justice, just what the account-book of our life looks like — the account-book of our Torah and our good deeds — how woeful our shame and disgrace will be!

A man may be tempted to argue there, "I was always so busy, burdened and distracted". They will open the account-book at once and show him how many hours and days he managed to squander on idle chatting, evil gossip, slanderous and mocking talk. Had he only considered at the time that the lack and the defect he was thus creating could never be rectified and made up, that the wrong he was doing could never be made right — would he not have changed his course?

37

BASIC SPIRITUAL NECESSITIES FIRST

Two poor men were once walking along the road — penniless beggars who always made the rounds to gather charity, to keep body and soul together. It was a bitterly cold winter's day, and they were dressed in nothing but torn and patched rags, with holes in their worn-out shoes, so that the cold literally froze them to the bone. Furthermore, they were very hungry, having found nothing to eat for a very long time.

As they were walking, a magnificent coach driven by four handsome horses came riding by. They looked up and saw one of the prominent rich men of the neighborhood inside, accompanied by the members of his family, all dressed in splendid clothes, with the women adorned with precious jewels — rings, bracelets and necklaces whose flashing brilliance was literally blinding.

"Did you see that?" one of the beggars asked the other. "Did you see all that wealth and opulence? I tell you: if the good Lord ever helped me and gave me wealth like that, with such a fine coach and horses, and such lovely clothing and jewels, I would be a happy man. I would feel the grandest, most magnificent man in the world!"

"What a great big fool you are", said the other beggar. "Here you go getting grandiose ideas, wanting things that are far beyond you, that you haven't a chance to ever see in your life. Look at the terrible, frightful condition we are in right now, shivering with cold and starving to death. You would do better to pray to the blessed Lord for a loaf of bread and a bowl of soup to fill your stomach, and a warm coat to cover your body, and maybe a pair of good, sturdy shoes for your poor wounded feet. What business do you have hoping for gold and jewels and a small fortune?"

Every morning we go to the synagogue and pray, "We beseech Thee, Lord our God, make the words of Thy Torah pleasant in our mouth... so that we and our offspring... may all know Thy name and learn Thy Torah for its own sake". Yet at that moment, how many of us are so very, very far removed not only from the study of Torah for its own sake, but even from such elementary matters of religious observance as never shaving with a razor, never eating non-kosher food, and so forth — forbidden practices that people trample underfoot in their scorn.

While such people, and all the more certainly their children, are utterly "naked and barefoot" spiritually, having not even these basic mitzvoth to their credit, it is so necessary for them to beseech the blessed Lord not for the silver, gold and precious jewels of Torah study for its own sake, but first and foremost for a "garment" to cover their spiritual nudity: that they should become worthy to live as observant Jews, following the path of the Torah and fulfilling its mitzvoth.

Only afterward will it be fitting and well for them to pray for the beautiful spiritual adornment of learning Torah for its own sake.

38
THE LIST OF TASKS

There are a great many people whose prayer and Torah study are nothing more than habit, something done by rote. Their grandfather used to pray three times a day and study Torah for a set period every day; and their father did the same. They too were educated in Torah and prayer, and became accustomed to it. So they continue, pulled along by force of habit; but for the most part their ears do not hear at all the sounds of study and prayer that their mouths produce.

This can be illustrated by a parable:

A penniless man once came to a very wealthy man and begged him for employment. Otherwise, he said, he would simply perish from hunger. The rich man took pity on him and hired him to work in the house: The poor man was to be his personal attendant, always to attend to his needs.

The time came when the rich man had to leave his home for an extended trip that would keep him away for quite a few days. He called over this new personal attendant of his and gave him a sheet of paper. "Here", he said, "take this sheet. I have written out clearly, in detail, all the things you have to do while I am away. Make sure to read this sheet every day, so that you won't go and forget something among the tasks that I have given you."

The time for his return came, and when he was back again and comfortably seated in his study, he sent for his personal attendant. "Well", he asked, "did you look after everything as I told you, while I was away?"

"O yes, sir", the man replied. "Several times a day, every day, I read carefully through that sheet of paper that you gave me."

"And . . ." said his employer.

"And what, sir?"

"And did you carry out all the tasks I wrote on that piece of paper?"

The poor personal attendant looked at him in bewilderment: "Wha...wha...what, sir?"

"You total idiot", cried the rich man angrily. "Did you think I gave you that sheet of paper only that you should have something to read? The whole point was that you should be able to remember all the things you had to do while I was away. What good could it do me if you just read the piece of paper over and over?"

Well, think now of those people who study Torah and pray daily by nothing more than force of habit. Does their behavior make any more sense? They go to the prayer-services every day and recite the *Sh'ma* morning and evening. And with that, they fondly imagine, they have done their duty. Yet this is nonsense. The *Sh'ma* is only like that sheet of paper which the wealthy man left with his personal attendant. It lists the various tasks and duties that we have to carry out, being under a timeless command to do them, that we received from the blessed Lord, the Divine Master of the world.

Then if people come along and act like that foolish personal attendant, being satisfied just to read the orders of their Divine Employer, what in the world do they accomplish?

39
THE CHOICE OF MERCHANDISE

A certain Jew once failed miserably in business, and try as he might, he found no way of earning a living in his home town. Unable to sit idle and watch his family suffer hunger and the humiliation of grinding poverty, he decided to go overseas and try his luck in a distant land. Off he went to the nearest seaport and took passage on a ship about to sail. As it happened, the ship was headed for Africa, and there he landed and settled.

As he looked about him, he noted that the natives had no livestock of sheep or cows, probably because there was very little land suitable for pasture. But he was familiar with dairy farming, and he believed that in the hot African climate, milk and dairy products could easily become popular. He imported a few cows from a neighboring country, raised a good crop of fodder for them on a field that he acquired, and began selling his dairy products. As he prospered, his herd of cows increased, and in a few years he was quite well-to-do.

From the start he corresponded with his wife, sending her small sums of money every week. Finally a letter arrived from her, to tell him that "your daughters are now grown, and they are of an age for marriage. Heaven has blessed your way in life, and you have gathered wealth. Then it would be only right and proper for you to return, and allot handsome dowries for your daughters, so that they can find good husbands from fine families."

As his wife was clearly right, he began to make plans to leave and return home. But then he thought, "Shall I just take back with me all the money I have made? There is no profit in that. My money won't be worth any more there than it is here. A hundred thousand dollars are always a hundred thousand dollars, never more. I would do better to take merchandise and sell it there." And what better merchandise could he take, he thought fatuously, than the same thing that was so successful here? He would take along plain cold milk. That always sold well, he told himself. Sure. . . .

On the ship that would take him back he loaded his cargo: barrel after barrel of milk. Then he sent his wife a letter telling her what he had done and asking her to meet him at the port upon his arrival.

There was still an hour or two before his ship would sail, and he went into town to see if there were perhaps some last-minute purchases to make before he took off for home.

As he walked along the street he met a friend who dealt in gold and precious stones. "Well, well", said his friend, "so you are sailing home. You know, you really cannot go without buying some presents for your wife and daughters. Come, pick out a lovely ring, a bracelet, a necklace. Here I have some exquisite things."

"Oh, nonsense", said the man, with a shrug of contempt. "As I have plenty of money I can always buy anything I want wherever I am. Why buy these trinkets here and carry them with me all the way home? I would rather buy some merchandise that I can resell there at a profit."

His friend did his best, though, to convince him that it would pay to buy the jewelry here, since such things cost very little here, being in plentiful supply, while in Europe they were very expensive. With another shrug the man consented, picked out some jewels, and then found it was time to return to the ship.

When the vessel landed, there were surprises in store for him. First, not only his wife and daughters waited for him, eager to see him after a separation of years. All his old friends and townspeople were there, to give him a royal welcome, having heard how wealthy he had become while abroad. It was a joyous occasion, with everyone embracing him and shaking his hand warmly.

Soon he saw the cargo being unloaded, and he went to claim his barrels of milk. And now another surprise awaited him — but a nasty one. From afar he could already detect the powerful stench. The entire shipment of milk had turned rancid, and so terrible was the stench that people could hardly go near the barrels. There was nothing to be done but to dump the entire shipment into the sea. . . . In utter despair the man watched his entire savings, all he had earned and saved in his years abroad, going down with those barrels to the bottom of the ocean. He had left this country a poor man. He now returned to it a poor man.

When his wife grasped what had happened, she began wringing her hands and crying bitterly at her calamitous fate. She could only see all her dreams shattered before her. How would they live? How would they ever marry off their daughters? "What cruel fate", she cried, "gave me such an addled idiot for a husband? You could not find any other merchandise to bring here, but only milk? We lack milk here? We need to get it from Africa? Every farmer around us gets more milk from his cows than he knows what to do with. The sun there must have gone to your head. Instead of sinking all your money into milk, why could you not buy gold and jewels? Then every daughter of ours could have had a good dowry and could have found herself a fine husband!"

Miserable and wretched as he felt, the man looked up with a start. His wife's words rang a bell, reminding him of the jewels he had bought from his friend in Africa before boarding ship. Without a word he went to his traveling case and found the precious objects; then off he went to the local jeweler and sold them, receiving enough money to support the family for several years.

The spirit of a man gets born with a physical body into this lowly world, and he finds himself well supplied with milk, butter, cheese... all kinds of food. Food is important in this world, necessary to keep a person alive. So a human being imagines that in all the world there is no merchandise more worthy than that, and he decides to invest all his energy and money and resources to acquire food. He works to keep his physical body well fed, and pays no attention to the spiritual gold and jewelry that are practically rolling underfoot and can be acquired with such little effort, at such little cost.

Wherever we turn, whatever we do, there is Torah to be learned; there are mitzvoth to be kept. And when we bring such "merchandise" to the world of truth, the Hereafter, we will find that they are worth more than the finest gold and jewels. Yet when a human being's appointed time comes and he must depart this world to return "home", what "merchandise" does he take with him? He takes to the grave a body that was fed, all his years on earth, with milk and butter and cheese; that was stuffed with fine foods and delicacies of every kind. Like that fatuous simpleton who sailed home from Africa, he takes things that he believes have great value at his place of arrival. He travels confidently with his cargo, expecting to become "wealthy" upon his arrival, only to find that his merchandise has all turned rancid and foul.

He arrives there, and at the port of entry, the heavenly court of justice, he is asked: "Well, what have you brought with you? You know, you have come from a land of gold and precious stones — Torah and mitzvoth. Did you bring a large supply with you?" And there he will stand, hanging his head in shame, pointing to his cargo: the great load of milk, etc. that he brought — which by now has become thoroughly spoiled and rancid, exuding a vile stench, so that it is fit only for the worms and maggots to eat.

Well, as the human spirit stands there, suffused in mortal shame, he will suddenly recall that once, absent-mindedly, he gave a poor beggar a few pennies. At a certain dinner, in order to make a good impression on his neighbors, he gave a modest donation to a yeshivah. Once there had even been an appeal in the synagogue on behalf of a Torah scholar in unfortunate circumstances; and in a moment of weakness he pledged (and later gave) a fair sum. In short, he realizes now that without attaching too much importance to it he did buy and bring with him a few valuable "bits of jewelry".

Of course, he will get full value for his few fine pieces of gold and jewels. But imagine his anguish and mortification at the thought that he could have brought such a great fortune with him, if only he had had the sense to know which "merchandise" to acquire.

40
TO PREPARE GOOD DEFENSE ATTORNEYS

A man lives his life, as a rule, involved in the cares of his workaday world. He must forever hurry and scurry, because time is money, and he is always in need of money to fill his stomach and take care of his worldly, physical needs. The only trouble is that in all his busy, dizzy activity in his business world, a man forgets that the day will come when he must stand before the heavenly court of justice, to receive a verdict of punishment or mercy. Whatever the verdict will be, harsh or kind, it will be for all time. Life in the Hereafter goes on perpetually, beyond the boundaries of time.

As he stands trial before that great court of heaven, a man will find angels of all sorts coming to testify about him: evil angels (demons) created by his sins and misdeeds, will come to accuse and denounce him. Good, benign angels created by the mitzvoth he kept will come and testify in his favor, defending him stoutly.

Let a man remember that the favorable outcome of his heavenly trial will depend on the nature of the defense he receives from the good angels. We can explain it with an illustration: Suppose a man is under arrest and about to go on trial for his life, facing very serious charges. It is self-understood that he will seek the very best defense attorney he can find, and will be ready to pay any fee, as long as he can know for certain that his lawyer can stand up to any prosecuting attorney and persuade the judges to believe in his innocence. If, however, the defendant has no concern to find a good man to defend him, and he engages a lawyer who stammers and stutters and makes a very poor appearance in court, whereas the prosecution brings its most capable attorneys to court, the man can obviously expect a death sentence from the start.

So amid our hurrying and scurrying on the face of the earth, trying to earn and amass our bit of money, we would do well to remember that a trial awaits us — a trial of eternal life or death. Now, while we are alive, we have the opportunity to engage good defense attorneys to speak for us at the heavenly court. We can get the very best defense attorneys — through Torah study, prayer and the performance of mitzvoth. Only, we must bear in mind that the Torah must be studied, the prayer said, and the mitzvoth done in holiness and purity, with proper concentration and intention. Then the good angels that we thus create will be strong and "healthy"; they will speak well for us, and their words will be heard in the heavenly court of justice. And then we can rest content and secure that we will receive a favorable verdict, of eternal life in the world-to-come.

41
IN ORDER OR DISORDER

Sometimes, if rarely, we find a shopkeeper who keeps his store in total disorder. His merchandise is simply thrown about everywhere, in every corner, under tables and counters. On the shelves nothing is arranged by any kind of system. He makes no attempt to separate fine expensive goods from plain cheap wares, worth only pennies, being thoroughly lazy and careless. As a result, a great deal of his merchandise becomes spoiled or simply gets lost.

Consider by contrast a storekeeper who is orderly and methodical. He knows the place and the value of every article, even of the lowest quality. Every kind of goods has its own section, and the shelves are a model of order. Thus even the plainest item finds its customers and has its sale.

We can find an analogous situation in the worship of the Lord:

The wise man has his eyes in his head. He takes care about his daily actions, that all should be done for the sake of Heaven. And the result is that he manages to do his mitzvoth, his religious good deeds, in good order, with good sense and taste. For example, if he pays his workers their wages promptly, he bears in mind during the process that he is thus fulfilling the Divine commandment, *On the same day you shall give him his hire* (Deuteronomy 24:15). So he gains the merit for a great mitzvah, for something which others, who pay scant attention to mitzvoth, regard as of no consequence. And if he does the same thing with every action of his, bearing in mind wherever possible that with an act of his he means to fulfill a commandment of the Lord — he thus fills his heavenly shop with all kinds of good spiritual merchandise: package upon package of mitzvoth and good acts, each neatly set and arranged in its place. When he appears before heaven's court of justice he will present every article of his spiritual wares, everything in its place; and he will receive full reward.

Others, though, trample such matters underfoot. They too perform mitzvoth by their ordinary actions and ways of behavior. In their heavenly store, however, everything is in complete disorder, lying in utter disarray, in damaged or second-hand condition.

42

AS GOOD AS IN THE HAND

When a Jew walks in the ways of the Lord, keeping the Torah and observing its mitzvoth from morning till night, he ought to be constantly in a mood of great happiness, even if he lives in pressing, straitened circumstances and his material condition in this world is never good.

Let us explain with a parable: A certain poor man had a stroke of fortune and found he was to get a large sum of money. He rushed home at once, to tell his wife and children about it. Their happiness was even greater than his, and the home rang with the sounds of their rejoicing. His wife and children were beside themselves with elation, and their singing and dancing for joy could be heard in the street.

People passing by stopped and wondered: What was this poor, needy family so happy about? They rarely had a decent meal to eat. Filled with curiosity, the people went in to ask about it. Of course, the explanation was simple enough: The indigent man had won a very big prize in the national lottery. He held out his lottery ticket and shouted that from now on he would be a wealthy man. He was finished with poverty.

"Well, that all may be true," said one of the visitors, "but right now you do not have two pennies to jingle together in your pocket. You haven't food enough in the house for a decent meal. Why such great elation now, already?"

"What sort of fool are you?" the poor man retorted. "As long as I have the ticket with the winning number, the money is as good as in my pocket. I only have to go and collect it. Tomorrow I plan to ride over to the lottery office and receive it. So I certainly have reason to celebrate right now."

We know well that a poor man's life is bad. It is hard to bear the distress of poverty and need. Yet if in spite of that a person fulfills mitzvoth by his own hand, sets fixed hours for his Torah study, and walks in the path of the Lord — in that way he becomes (as it were) the winner of a large prize in the lottery, with a fortune awaiting him in the Hereafter. That good reward is reserved and guaranteed for him. However long he will yet live, it will be as a few days compared to the eternity that follows. Thus "in a few days" he will receive his great reward. Is it then not right and proper for him to be constantly filled with a mood of great happiness?

43
WHILE THE KING IS HERE

Scripture commands us to "cling to Him" (Deuteronomy 11:22). We have to realize how fortunate we are, how exalted is our lot in this world, that we have been given the ability to cling to the blessed Lord and be attached to Him. This great privilege is available to a human being only as long as he is alive on this earth — by keeping the Torah and its mitzvoth. Once he expires, however, and reaches the world of truth in the Hereafter, there are already many partitions and interferences between him and the Holy Blessed One. He can no longer draw near to Him and cling to Him.

Let us explain with a parable: The owner of an inn prospered so much that he aroused the envy of impecunious neighbors, who wished to remove him and gain possession of the inn. They went to certain government officials and made false accusations against him, giving bribes to the "right" people to make sure they would be believed. Without bothering to call the innkeeper and question him, the official court of the emperor sentenced him to life imprisonment at hard labor.

The astounded man went into action, to move heaven and earth in an attempt to save himself. He hired the most noted attorneys in the land. He sent people who knew the court judges, to intercede and speak for him. He left no stone unturned — and got nothing for his pains. It was all in vain. The sentence could not be changed or removed.

Yet his friends told him not to despair. "There is still one more thing to do," they told him. "We see now that nothing else can help, but you must go and present yourself to the emperor alone. It is well known that he is fair and merciful, and will always listen to the plea of one of his subjects. If you can only succeed in convincing him of your innocence, you can be sure that he won't let any injustice be done to you."

Now, the emperor had a custom that once a year he took off his royal garments and dressed in ordinary clothing, and thus he went wandering and traveling about in the land, letting no one know that he was the sovereign ruler. In this way he wished to have a good look at life and events in his country, to see if all was going along properly, or if perhaps some blatant injustice was going on and people were suffering needlessly.

By a stroke of fate, his travels brought him to the town of the innkeeper, and one night he came to stay at the inn. No one had the least idea, however, of who he really was. Only a few days after he left did the secret manage to leak out.

Well, when the innkeeper learned that the emperor himself had been there, he was beside himself with vexation and grief. Here he was in desperate need of seeing the sovereign ruler and talking to him, to plead his case and convince the emperor of his innocence; the man had been at his inn, sleeping the night, having his meals; he could have spoken to him, face to face, and the emperor would have listened. And the opportunity was gone, slipped through his fingers.

He began tearing his clothing and shouting in agony, "Woe is me, woe is me! The great merciful emperor came right here, to my inn. I could have pleaded my case and implored him for mercy. And I missed the chance! How will I ever get to him now? He is locked away in his palace, guarded by hundreds of sentries without and within, who make sure that no uninvited guest can ever get in to see him."

This is exactly what happens with human beings on earth. While they are here, in this lowly world, He is present and available (if we may so speak). The supreme King of kings, the Holy Blessed One is in the home of every Jew. There can be no better opportunity to approach Him (as it were) to pour out our prayer and beseech Him for all our needs, be it in regard to children, health or money matters. Yet how many simply miss the golden opportunity and let their great chance slip away. When they want to see Him in His heavenly mansion, in the Hereafter, it is no longer so easy at all. It is very doubtful if they can ever succeed there in drawing close to Him.

Let every single member of Jewry bear this well in mind, so that he will know how to use his moments of opportunity, while the Divine Sovereign is with him, at his inn.

44
THE WORTHLESS BARGAINS

When the son of a certain wealthy man reached an age to marry, his father arranged for him to take a wife, giving the young couple a handsome cash settlement and promising them support for the next few years. When those few years ended, his father called the young man to him. "My son", said he, "the time has come for you to stand on your own two feet. You shall have to learn how to earn a living. Take the money I gave you at your marriage, as a cash settlement; go among people in the marketplace, and try your hand at buying and selling merchandise. Make sure, though, to consider well what sort of commodities you wish to choose, to trade in them."

A trade fair was opening in a nearby town, and with the money securely in his pocket, the young man set off for it. He went through the town to find the market square, and there he went about among the large stands and displays of merchandise, noting everything carefully. One stand especially caught his eye: He saw whole shelves filled with vessels and objects made, as it seemed to him, of gold. Ah, he thought, housewares of gold! They must surely be worth buying, if the price was right. He stepped close.

"Tell me", he asked the owner, "how much do you want for these wares of gold?" The owner gave the young man a shrewd look and realized with whom he was dealing. "Hmm", he began. "These objects are of pure gold, you know. They are worth a small fortune. Yet in spite of that I will let you have them for very little. I am in need of cash; and besides, I like to give a fine young man like you a chance to get ahead in the world. If you won't hesitate, you have an opportunity here to make a handsome profit."

Flushed with flattery and ambition, the young man paid the price, half of his father's cash settlement. When the objects of "pure gold" were neatly wrapped, he left the package safely at the hotel where he was staying; and he then returned to the fair in search of more "bargains", feeling that this was his lucky day. This time he was attracted to some elaborately printed government bonds, due to earn large interest in several months, that were being offered at a very big discount — again because their owner was supposedly in need of ready cash. There was only one small drawback, of which our young man was blissfully unaware: they were forgeries. With the second half of his money he bought them, and returned home in happiness.

When his father saw the "bargains", his face mirrored his dismay.

The vessels and objects were of cheap metal covered with gold paint, worth not a fraction of what the young man had paid for them. Half the money had gone down the drain over them. "Woe is me", he cried. "How could you just give away so much money without examining what you were buying?"

"It is all right, father", replied the young man, recovering from the blow. "I can make up the loss and still show a profit. Wait till you see what I bought with the rest of the money: first-class government bonds."

"Very well; let us see them." The young man drew them from his wallet and put them on the table. But his father needed only one look to tell him the truth: "You fool! What have you done? Look at that smudged printing. Could you not tell that these are forgeries? For months the Treasury officials have been scouring the country, looking for the counterfeiters who made these, and the dealers who go about peddling them. Now you have really made a fine mess of things. Not only is the money gone, vanished like the snows of yesteryear. The Treasury officials may trace those papers to us, and we may have to stand trial for dealing in forged government bonds! Do you realize how absolutely stupid you have been? Just see how you let two swindlers fleece you. Here I thought that with the money I gave you, you would show valor and astute judgment, and become a man. And you went and acted like a nincompoop. You are left without money, and you face a prison sentence!"

From the moment of his birth, a man has a fine "cash settlement" allotted him by the blessed Lord: so many years of life, and so much income to support himself — so that he can make it his business to study Torah and observe the mitzvoth, thus to earn his share of life in the world-to-come. Yet what does many a person do? Not only does he fail to make any honest effort to earn enough merit for his spiritual sustenance in the world-to-come; not only does he do no "profitable business" with the "cash settlement" that the blessed Lord allotted him. Like that foolish young man, he goes and loses his precious resources of life by "bad business", by investing them in absolute nonsense: flashy, trashy baubles of life that glitter like gold; valuable certificates of solid worth, that in the Hereafter, the world of truth, turn out to be forgeries, the ink on them running at the first drop of water.

How many human beings manage to exchange the truly valuable allotment of the blessed Lord — life-energy and the time to study Torah and do mitzvoth — for worthless trivia and evil business. They commit sins and flaunt their disobedience of the will of the world's Divine Sovereign.

The time comes when such a man must face his Father in heaven, after his departure from life on earth. "My son", He will ask (if we may so speak), "in what did you trade, with the 'cash settlement' that I gave you?" And he will take out his "golden vessels" made of cheap metal with gilt paint, and his counterfeit government bonds — the meretricious nonsense on which he spent his life. What else can we expect the Divine Father to do but grow enraged at this foolish waste of something so immensely valuable?

45
THE VERY HAPPIEST DAY

Out hunting one day, a royal prince found himself trapped in quick-sand. He would have perished, had not a poor man come along in the nick of time. Dressed in rags, suffering hunger and thirst, with not a penny to his name, the poor man had a stout walking stick; and this he held out to the sinking prince, so that the young man could take hold and pull himself out.

The prince insisted on taking the poor man with him back to the royal palace, where he presented the ragged beggar to his father, the king. "I owe you a great measure of thanks", said the sovereign, "for saving my son's life. This is what I shall do: I will grant you permission to go into my treasure-rooms for a day. For one whole day you may move about there freely and take whatever you wish. Whatever you can take with you is yours. Remember, though: you will have exactly one day, and no more."

Early the next day the beggar came, to be escorted by a royal guard to the treasure-rooms in the palace, where the doors were flung open to him. We can imagine with what eagerness he fell upon the sacks of gold pieces, the collections of jewels and precious stones. As swiftly as he could, he began stuffing his pockets and filling the few sacks he had brought with him, hardly knowing where to turn first. At the end of the day he left, laden with as much as he could carry, and warmed by the knowledge that he was now one of the richest men in the land.

In a few days all traces of his poverty were gone. He was now the well-dressed owner of a fine house, with a staff of servants; and he began looking about to decide how and where it would be most profitable for him to invest his wealth. Soon he found that his money was earning far more money for him, and he became fabulously wealthy, with one of the greatest fortunes in the world.

From the start, he established an annual custom for himself: Every year, on the anniversary of the fortuitous event that changed the course of his life from rags to great riches, he would make a great, fine feast, to which he invited all the high government officials and noblemen, and the most distinguished citizens of the land. It was always a happy occasion, where everyone rejoiced and made merry.

For many years he continued the practice, until, with the passage of time, no one remembered what the original reason was for this splendid annual feast. No one remembered how the man had originally risen to wealth. It seemed to all that he had always been vastly rich, with business holdings that remained successful. . . . One year, though, in the midst of the annual banquet, as all the distinguished guests sat enjoying themselves at the laden table, the wealthy man decided to speak:

"Gentlemen", he said, when all had grown silent, "let me ask you something." They turned their attention to him. "Which day of my life, do you think, was the happiest of all?"

They may have expressed it in different ways, but all gave essentially the same answer: "It must have been one of these days when you make your annual banquet. It is such a happy, festive time for us all. This banquet hall is sumptuously decorated. The tables are laden with every kind of delicacy. The setting are of shining silver and gold. The china is the finest. Servants attend upon us hand and foot. The company is of the most distinguished people in the land. The food is superb, and there is lavish entertainment. And here you sit, relaxed and happy in this genial atmosphere. How, where could you be happier?"

Their host only laughed. "No, gentlemen," he said; "you are mistaken. It was quite a different kind of day that was the happiest and most wonderful in my life. I remember it clearly, as though it was yesterday. I was desperately poor then, dressed in rags, and ravenously hungry. Not only were there no servants to wait upon me, but I ranked then lower than any servant. And yet, every moment of that day I was filled with a boundless indescribable joy." All the guests looked at him in astonishment, unable to make any sense out of his words.

"That", their host continued, "was the day our king opened all his treasure-rooms to me and allowed me to take anything my heart desired — but only on that one day. It was my reward for having saved his son's life. I was extremely hungry and thirsty, and tired. Do you think I paid any attention to that? I never felt or noticed any hunger, thirst or fatigue. Dressed in rags as I was, I was delirious with joy, knowing that with every passing moment I was becoming richer and richer. I had eyes only for the treasures all about me. I could think of nothing else — only to take more and more. Whatever happened, I knew I must not lose a minute of that precious day. I stuffed my pockets and filled my bags, with a contentment growing and spreading in my heart. Not once that day did I suffer or worry over hunger or thirst. . . . That, gentlemen, was the most perfectly happy day of my life. For me there has never been a day like it, either before or afterward."

What is this mundane world of ours? It is the Almighty's treasure-house, filled with His priceless Torah and mitzvoth. He has opened wide its doors for us, allowing us to go in and gather everything good that we desire — but this permission is only for one day: the short period of our stay on earth, from the sunrise of birth to the sunset of our passage to another world.

Whoever understands what immense good fortune awaits him here, will take and gather as much as he can from the treasures about him, the wonderful opportunities for spiritual achievement. He will let not a moment go to waste, knowing that any time lost will never return to him. And he will know that the minutes and hours he spends at this are the most wonderful and joyous of his life. He will feel neither hunger nor thirst. It will not bother him if his clothes are torn and ragged. For him there is one goal and purpose: to gather treasure — Torah learning, mitzvoth and good deeds.

Too many persons, though, think like the guests at the banquet of that wealthy man. They think that the very happiest time in a man's life is when he sits at a splendid feast, eating and drinking his fill, with servants dancing attendance.

In the ultimate future, however, the blessed Lord will remove the blinders from our heart and eyes. Then all will see and realize that they are in His treasure-rooms, with the precious right to gather what they can. Then all will be "learned of the Lord" and His Divine knowledge will fill the consciousness of all mankind with its golden radiance

46
THE COMFORTABLE WRONG-WAY JOURNEY

Two youngsters, both gifted students, went together for many years to the same Torah school. Then their paths in life separated: One went on to a famous Torah academy in another city, where he applied himself to his studies, persevering zealously until he became a fine young scholar, and his instructors, who held him in high regard, ordained him as a rabbi. The second youngster, however, went on to secular studies and took up, eventually, the study of medicine, until he received his medical degree. In the process, though, he threw off all allegiance to the Jewish faith, and would have nothing more to do with the Torah and its mitzvoth.

The first young man became the rabbi of a small town in Poland, that could afford to pay him only a minimal salary, barely enough to live on. The second became a qualified physician in private practice, and was soon earning handsome fees.

Once the young rabbi was called to a neighboring town to help decide a very complicated dispute between two people that was being judged there at the *beth din,* the local religious court. As it happened, an elderly man in that same neighboring town was taken very ill, and the young doctor was called in to treat him. When the rabbi finished at the *beth din,* having heard the case and given his decision, and the physician finished treating the sick man, the two went to return to their homes, and they met on the street. Overjoyed at seeing each other again after so many years, they fell to talking, each telling the other all that had happened with him since their old schooldays together.

When the young doctor heard how little his childhood friend was earning, how hard it was for him to make ends meet, he said, "Just look: we were friends, learning in one schoolroom, and we were equally good at our studies. Now see where I have reached in the world, and where you have arrived. I am a doctor and earn good fees; I never have to worry about money, and can live very comfortably. You serve as a rabbi, and you earn so little that you have to live in near-poverty. Decide for yourself: Would you not have done better to take my road in life?"

The young rabbi smiled: "Let me tell you something that happened to me only today. When I finished my business in this town, I wanted to start back home, and I went to hire the driver of a horse-and-wagon to take me there. Since I live a good distance away, the driver asked for ten dollars. As I was about to agree reluctantly, not having any real choice, a man who stood at the side listening interrupted excitedly: 'Just a minute, rabbi. Why should you pay ten dollars to ride in that rickety old wagon? Let me show you a fine coach drawn by four splendid horses; and the trip in that won't cost you more than three dollars!'

"I discovered only later that the man was simply a sharpster. A rich person arrived in the town this morning in that coach, and he would have to return home in any case. There was plenty of room in his coach, and he would be glad for a bit of company. If I rode home with him, there would be no reason in the world to pay anyone anything. At the time, though, I knew nothing of this, and I was grateful for this man's offer. We went off together at once, to find this handsome coach with the four horses.

"Well, it was just as he said: There was indeed a fine coach harnessed to four magnificent horses, about to leave the town. There was indeed room within it for me, and I was welcome to ride along. It would be a most comfortable trip for a very small price. There was only one difficulty: Instead of heading for my home town, it was about to take off in the opposite direction.

"Now just imagine what would have happened to me, had I listened to that sharpster and ridden off in the fine coach. For a while I would have enjoyed traveling so comfortably in high style. Then, sooner or later, I would have learned of my mistake. I would have had to get off that splendid coach and traveled back the way I had come — in a plain, rickety horse-and-wagon. It would have cost me more than the ten dollars which this wagon-driver asked; and I would have needed half a day to recover from a long bumpy ride like that.

"There, my friend (the rabbi concluded), you have the difference between you and me. This world, you know, is like a great trade fair. Everything is available. Every man can buy precious goods and take them home with him. Well, I make a meager living, and even that with difficulty. It costs me great toil and hardship to acquire Torah learning now and do a few mitzvoth properly. Today I have to ride home in a plain, broken-down wagon. It is hard to sit in it, and the travel will be back-breaking. Yet I can be sure that it is taking me, with the mitzvah I acquired today by coming here, along the right road, to bring me to my true destination. And that, my friend, is how I am traveling through life.

"You, of course, have set off on your journey in life in a splendid upholstered coach, wide and comfortable. There are no difficulties, no worries.... There is only one trouble, though: It is not taking you home. It is going altogether in the wrong direction. In the end you will have to go back. You will have to return into the world in another lifetime, to undergo untold suffering and hardship so as to undo and atone for all that you are doing wrong in this lifetime. Only then will you be able to arrive home — to your proper place of eternal tranquillity in the Hereafter."

This is what Scripture conveys when it says, *What gain does a man have from all his toil at which he labors under the sun?* (Ecclesiastes 1:3). If all the toil and work of a man is only of the kind that remains "under the sun" — if he labors only to provide for his needs and ambitions in this world, never giving a thought to the needs and wishes he will have in the world-to-come — what is the good of all his toil and labor? What gain or profit will remain with him at the end? His journey through life will be comfortable and pleasurable; but he will find that he has traveled the wrong way.

47
THE UNUSED LOAN

One day a rich man went walking through the streets of the city, when he met a poor man who knew him. "Do me a favor", said the poor man. "Lend me five thousand dollars."

"Do you think it right for me to let you have such a large sum? There are poor people coming to me every day to ask for help. The most I ever give, as a rule, when a needy man asks for a loan, is two hundred dollars. So with five thousand dollars I could help twenty-five persons. Why should I give you the whole amount and others nothing?"

"Look", the other began to plead. "You know me. You know I used to be wealthy until my luck changed and I lost everything. If you will let me have the money, I have a chance now to get back on my feet. There is a very good business that I could get into. Then I would not need any more charity...."

"That", said the rich man, "is a different story. In that case, I will make an exception to my rule. Come to my house this evening, and you can have your loan."

In a year it was time for the poor man to repay his debt. He came to the rich man and gave him an envelope containing five thousand dollars. But the wealthy man recognized the package: It was the very same envelope, with the same package of bills, that he had given the poor man a year ago!

"What is this?" he asked in some anger. "Did you just take the money and hold on to it for a year? You put it away in a drawer and forgot about it? I only gave it to you because you pleaded that you had a chance to go into business again. The money was of no help to you, and you simply prevented me from using it to help other people. How could you do something so despicable?"

The blessed Lord infused a living holy spirit into us, a precious treasure beyond price. With it we can "do business" in the world. We can learn the Torah and keep its mitzvoth faithfully. Yet what do we tend to do in our foolishness? We leave this precious treasure in some forgotten corner, and do not use it at all.

What will we do when the time comes to return this treasure to its Divine owner, and He will see that we never used it at all, never derived any benefit from it? How are we going to explain it?

48
THEY TRAVELED FOR NOTHING

A trade fair came to an end in a Polish city, and a whole group of Jewish merchants and businessmen went riding home together. Among them were wholesalers, who had a large trade, buying and selling in quantity; and there were retailers, small tradesmen. The large tradesmen had done very well at the fair, netting fine profits. But the small tradesmen had also not done badly, and had found the fair profitable enough for them.

As they rode home together, they took to talking and chatting among themselves, telling of their experiences at this fair that had just closed. Each told in turn what he had bought and sold, and how his affairs had gone.

One man, though, sat in the corner and kept silent. "Sir", someone finally asked him, "why don't you tell us how *you* did at the fair? What did *you* buy or sell? And did *you* make any money?"

"You must excuse me", he replied. "I am not a merchant at all. I did no trading at the fair, and am simply going just as I came, without a penny profit."

Everyone there began joking about him, making him a laughing-stock. "Imagine that", said one of them. "People wait months for a trade fair. They make all kinds of plans and careful preparations for it, knowing it is a valuable opportunity to reap profits — enough to live on for months. You spent time and money to come to the fair, and you did nothing there! You arrived poor and you left penni-less. . . ."

The man had his reasons, however, and he patiently explained to the others why he had taken this strange course. At last they under-stood, and stopped laughing and mocking him. With all that, though, he remained just as poor and penniless as before.

From the heavenly world of the spirit a man descends into this lowly world, which can be likened to a great trade fair. Then his proper purpose in coming here should be to "do business" for his spirit. There is a chance here to earn a spiritual fortune in Torah learning and mitzvoth. It is a rare opportunity, that will not come again. Woe to the man who lets it all go by.

Some spend their time in Torah study and become learned in re-ligious law. They thus do very well at the fair, and "return home" laden with immense spiritual profit. On the other hand, there are thoughtless fools who waste all their time at the fair, doing no "busi-ness" whatever; and they "return home" empty-handed.

When they arrive in the world of truth, in the Hereafter, all will mock them and deride them for their stupidity. They will become a laughing-stock. "Look at the opportunity you had", the others will say. "See how wealthy you could have become. And you let it all go by!" Of course, these persons will then try to defend themselves and explain why they failed to do any good business at the fair. Possibly they will succeed in giving a plausible explanation, that will be accepted. Yet what good will it do them? They will remain spiritually impov-erished, with no merit or virtue to their name.

49

BETTER INCALCULABLE REWARD THAN INCALCULABLE LOSS

In Scripture we read, *Come to Ḥeshbon* (Numbers 21:27); and the Sages interpret: Come, let us make *ḥeshbon*, the reckoning, of the world — the loss that a mitzvah entails, against its reward; and the reward that a sinful deed brings, against the loss it brings (Talmud, Bava Bathra 79).

At first sight this seems puzzling: What does a reckoning of the world have to do with the loss involved in a mitzvah and the reward gained from a misdeed?

Well, consider: If a man is endowed with the gift of rapid calculation, people may ask him how many grains of wheat are to be found in a bushel, and he will be able to come up with the correct answer. He may even be able to tell us how many grains of wheat it would take to fill a whole room. Yet who on earth would ever be able to answer this: If the entire world, from earth to sky, were filled with grains of wheat, and a bird ate one grain a month, how long would it take for the bird to eat up all the grains? No human calculation could begin to solve even a part of this problem.

Yet regarding any reckoning of the world, the earth, we must realize that it is like one small grain among the innumerable worlds that the Almighty has created. However vast this earth may be, it has a finite surface. However long a task on earth must take, it can only take a finite amount of time, which will be over some day. On the other hand, the Torah is timeless; every mitzvah brings a timeless reward, endowing a person with eternal life. And eternity is longer than whatever time a bird may need to eat all the grains that it would take to fill the entire world. Give the bird a long enough life, and sooner or later it must finish the task. Eternity never ends. It is time without limit or measure.

Let a man do one mitzvah, one religious good deed, and he gains eternal life. Let him commit one sinful deed, and he loses eternal life. Have we then the ability to make any reckoning of the reward for a mitzvah, compared with the loss that a wrongdoing brings? How can we calculate infinities?

This, then, is what the Sages mean: Just as we cannot make a reckoning about the entire world, although it is but one small grain among all the worlds, so is it a thousand times more certain that we cannot know how far the reward for a mitzvah reaches, or the loss suffered for a sin. The only wise thing to do is to earn a good share of life in eternity.

50
THE MISER

In a small town there once lived a miser. So very niggardly was he that he would even deprive himself of a fair ration of bread, and it was hard for him to allow himself a mouthful of proper food. His sole ambition in life was to save every possible penny, till he could amass a proper fortune, so that he could be ranked among the wealthy people of the town.

Our Sages said, however, that when a man has a hundred he wants two hundred. However much the miser managed to save, he never found it enough but always craved for more. So he thought one day: Who says that a man has to eat half a pound of meat a day? Why can I not get along on an eighth of a pound? In that way I can save a tidy sum during the year.

The year went by, and his amount of savings was indeed quite large. Still, a man like that could never be satisfied. Once again he began turning ideas over in his mind, looking for new ways to increase his hoard of savings. Finally he decided that the amount of bread he ate every day was also too much: he could make do with less. Needless to say, he was then able to save more money than before.

He felt that everything was going just fine, until one day he suddenly felt a great weakness in his heart. All at once he was left without an ounce of strength. His legs would no longer obey him: He found himself unable to walk up steps; and even when he went walking in the street, he found that he had to stop and rest from time to time, all out of breath. Frightened, he decided that he had to go and see a doctor.

"You seem to be in reasonably good health", said the doctor;

"only, you are suffering from what we call a general weakness and lack of blood. You have this condition in a very severe form; and in order to get well you will have to eat good, nourishing food. You will also need this medicine that I am prescribing for you. It is rather expensive, I am afraid. It costs about 200 dollars. But I don't think you have much choice if you want to get well."

Hearing this, the miser was so upset that he thought it would be the end of him. "Never mind", he murmured, "never mind. There must be some other way." And he groped and stumbled to find his way out of the doctor's office.

His illness only grew worse, however; and at times it seemed to him that he could already hear the wings of the angel of death, fluttering about his head. And it is well known that even the most miserly of misers is afraid of the angel of death.

So back he went to the doctor and pleaded with him to give him the prescription for that frightfully expensive medicine. In his desperation he was ready to buy it at any price.

"Now you have aroused my burning curiosity", said the doctor. "I just cannot give you the prescription until you tell me: What made you get so sick? In fact, how did you ever manage to become so very thin?"

The ailing miser told him everything, from the beginning to the end. And the doctor just laughed at him in scorn: "You idiot! How much money have you saved by stinting on your food? Two thousand dollars? three thousand dollars? It is going to cost you more than that now, with all the medicine and the special diet that you will need, to say nothing of the doctor's fees. And who knows if you will succeed in saving your life, considering how serious your condition is. It is possible that you have damaged your body beyond repair. Right now, only the good Lord knows..."

A man works and toils, struggles and strives. He deprives himself and his family of many beneficial things. He hardens his heart and is unable to give a poor man a few pennies. When charity collectors come, he does his best to avoid them. If a mitzvah is going to be expensive, he tried hard to evade doing it, or to do it in the cheapest way. He gives himself no rest, day or night, always driving himself toward the one goal of saving money. . . .

Perhaps it needs only one minute of his time, to allow him to stop and make a reckoning of his life. And perhaps then he won't make the same mistake as the miser.

III: THE SABBATH

51
JUST FASTER, NOT MORE

Suppose you were to go to a Jew who keeps his place of business open on the Sabbath, and you asked him, "Why do you do that? Do you not know what a serious wrong it is to violate the Sabbath? If a person does not observe the Sabbath, it is as though he denied the entire Torah. No matter how much profit you earn on this sacred day, is it really worthwhile for you to treat this precious treasure of ours with such brutal disregard?"

He would almost certainly reply, "What can I do? My needs and expenses are so high. There is an absolute minimum that I must earn every week, to pay the rent on this store, to feed my wife and children, to pay for their education, to buy them clothing, and so on and on. Sunday I am not allowed to open the store. How can I ever manage if I close the store two days a week?"

Yet there is a way to explain his fallacy, by an illustration: A simpleton once decided that since he was not getting enough hot water from his boiler, he would attach another faucet to it. With two faucets, he thought, he would get twice as much water. It never occurred to him that a second faucet would add no water to the boiler, but would merely draw out the heated water twice as fast.

The Divine Sovereign of the world sustains and provides for us all. For each and every one of His human beings He prepares rations of provisions, day by day, week by week. Everyone receives the measure that He allots — some an ample supply, and some a restricted supply. We can think of the weekly ration as a boiler of hot water with five or six faucets, each to provide its amount on one day of the week. Only a fool can believe that by adding an extra faucet he will receive an extra allotment of income from Heaven's grace.

A man's allotment by Divine providence remains the same, however. Then what does a Jew gain by desecrating the Sabbath?

52
THE SIGN ON THE SHOP

Every owner of a store or workshop, as a rule, hangs out a sign to announce his business, so that a man passing by in the street can know what he offers for sale. Moreover, as long as the sign hangs it indicates that the store or shop is still in business; the owner is still alive and in charge. He may have to close the place for a few days or weeks and go off on a trip; he may close up to take a vacation. As long as the sign hangs, though, it tells everyone that the place will remain in business. Should the sign be taken off, however, it is a clear indication, as good as the testimony of a hundred witnesses, that the owner has pulled up stakes and moved somewhere else, and left this location permanently.

The holy Sabbath is the sign of the Jew.

The Creator of the world established it as "a sign" between Him and us — a sign to attest that *in six days the Lord made heaven and earth, and on the seventh day He ceased from work and rested* (Exodus 31:17). Thus the Sabbath remains a clear sign and indication for every Jew, attesting that he is of our faith, loyal to the covenant, the holy bond, that the Holy Blessed One formed with the Jewish people. Even if by chance a Jew has transgressed and disobeyed one of the commandments of the Torah, he does not lose his Jewish identity by that. It is as though a storekeeper has left his shop for a while. For a short time, business was not conducted there; but the sign remained in place. As long as a Jew yet keeps the Sabbath as a sacred day of rest, refraining from all that the religious law forbids, he is still "in charge of the store"; he is still "in business" as a Jew.

Should someone take to desecrating the Sabbath, however (Heaven forbid), it is as if he took the sign off his shop. He attests by this that his spirit is no longer a Jewish soul. It has taken off and gone elsewhere — like a storekeeper who has removed the sign. This is why the Sages taught that if anyone violates the Sabbath, it is as though he has denied the entire Torah. He is "out of business" as a Jew.

53
THE THEFT THAT DOES NOT PAY

There was a rich Jew in Moscow who decided to "cheat" on the Almighty by "stealing" a bit of the Sabbath day. He used to keep his factory going past sunset on Friday; and Saturday evening, his night-shift of workers had to begin work before sunset.

When the Ḥafetz Ḥayyim heard about him, his only comment was a parable:

A certain farmer brought all the wheat that he raised to one particular Jewish merchant. Their arrangement was that whenever the farmer brought his sacks of wheat, they were to be weighed on the scales, and the merchant would make a mark on the wall for every measure (bushel) of wheat. After the harvest, the farmer and the merchant would count the marks together, so that they would know just how much wheat the farmer had brought, and how much money the merchant therefore owed him.

One day, however, the farmer decided that it was not a good system. Why, there was always the chance that the merchant might go and rub away a few of the marks on the wall. Every one of those marks was worth good money to him. No, he thought, it was too risky. So the next day he came to the merchant with another plan: For every measure of wheat that he brought, let the merchant put a coin into a dish that would be kept on a shelf. Then, at the end of the harvest, they would count the coins.

The merchant agreed; and as the farmer kept bringing his sacks of wheat, the dish on the shelf kept filling with coins. However, the sight of that money on the shelf was just too much for the simple farmer. Unable to resist temptation, when the merchant was not looking he reached up and took a handful of coins, and quickly slipped them into his pocket. Then off he went, happy as a lark at the thought of the money jingling in his pocket.

Of course, the merchant paid the farmer at the end of the season according to the number of coins in the dish. So the farmer paid dearly for his little "theft".

It is the same story (the Ḥafetz Ḥayyim concluded) with that rich man in Moscow. He is just as "clever" as that farmer. We are entirely dependent on the mercy of the blessed Lord, relying on Him to bestow His blessing on us. Well, He commanded us in His Torah, *Six days shall you labor and do all your work; but the seventh is a Sabbath to the Lord your God* (Exodus 20:9–10). And the Sages teach that through the Sabbath flows the beneficence and blessing by which the Divine providence sustains us. Then all that a man can earn during the other days of the week, derives from the Sabbath. If he "cheats" and steals away a few hours at its beginning and its end, he is cheating no one but himself. He is simply reducing the provision that Heaven bestows upon him on the weekdays.

IV: BETWEEN MAN AND HIS MAKER

54
THE NEEDLESS BURDEN OF WORRY

You can always find people going around bent under a load of worries, carrying a burden of uncertainty and anxiety: How will they ever manage to support their families? How will everything ever work out?...What has given them cause for worry? — They read in the newspaper, or so-and-so told them, that the times are getting really bad, and it is going to be very difficult to earn a living.

That kind of thinking is not particularly intelligent. Let us illustrate it with a parable:

A strong, mighty emperor ruled over many large and wealthy countries that were blessed with fertile soil and good natural resources. They produced enough food to support their population amply, and had enough left to export to other countries.

Once a group of villainous characters hatched a plot to overthrow the emperor and seize control of the country. The emperor learned of their intrigues in good time, however. He ordered the plotters placed under arrest and brought to trial as traitors to the royal empire.

On an afternoon before the trial began, the emperor went for a walk in the palace gardens. He looked up and saw a wonderfully beautiful bird on a tree, and its song was the sweetest he had ever heard. Filled with pleasure at the sight and sound of this exquisite winged creature, he called his servants and ordered them to capture it and put it in a large cage. They were then to leave the cage in one of the large drawing rooms of the palace, so that he would be able to see and hear the creature whenever his heart desired.

While the servants were busy carrying out the emperor's order, as they were about to get the lovely bird into the large cage, one of them gave a great sigh. "What is the matter?" the other servants asked him. "Why are you sighing like that?"

"It is such a pity", said the first servant. "I feel so sorry for this beautiful bird that it is to be condemned by fate to die of hunger in the emperor's palace."

The others looked at him in amazement: "Why will it die of hunger? Do you think it will be left without food in the palace?"

"Didn't you hear?" the first servant asked. "They uncovered a plot by a whole group of people to get rid of the emperor and seize power. At a time like this, who will have a clear mind to give a thought to one poor little bird, to give it food and water?"

The others laughed: "You are a great big fool. Just because a few hot-heads and desperate characters hatched a plot and dreamed a pipe-dream that they could make a successful rebellion against our powerful emperor, a sovereign ruler over vast, prosperous countries, you think he will forget to order one of us to feed it every day? Or do you think we won't find a few seeds every day to keep it well-fed?"

When people become obsessed and distracted with worry about having to earn a living, and their frantic efforts to increase their earnings darken their faces and their lives, let them keep this in mind. Let this be their answer when a small group of mindless heretics, philosophers of confusion, strive to turn their heart away from the path of the Lord, arguing that He cannot provide enough food for all who dwell on earth. Why should a few fools make us believe that we will fail to get the bit of food that we need for our daily sustenance? The Almighty remains in control.

55
THE HUFFING AND PUFFING DOES NOT HELP

A Jew in Warsaw who owned a small hotel learned that the Ḥafetz Ḥayyim was due to arrive in the city at a certain hour on a certain day. As that time approached, he went early to the railroad station and waited for the train to arrive. When he saw the pious sage getting off, he went over to welcome him, and invited the sage to stay at his hotel. The Ḥafetz Ḥayyim agreed.

As the two rode together to the hotel, the Ḥafetz Ḥayyim asked his host, "Tell me, dear sir: Do you have a set time for Torah study? How many hours a day are you able to devote to learning Torah? And exactly what are you studying?"

"*Oy vey*," the Jew sighed. "What can I tell you? Believe me, dear rabbi: my heart hurts me. But what can I do? I bear a heavy burden trying to earn my livelihood. I cannot tell you how hard it is. From early morning till late at night I am bothered and burdened. It is all hustle and bustle — till I finally get to bed late at night, without an ounce of strength left in me. You know, dear rabbi, Warsaw is a big city. Every hour there are trains arriving, bringing people; and I have to be there, at the railroad station, ready to welcome them and invite them to my hotel. Otherwise someone else will get to them ahead of me, and will invite them to his hotel; and I will lose out."

"You are making a big mistake", the Ḥafetz Ḥayyim answered him. "Forgive me for saying this, but you remind me of a certain country bumpkin who took a trip to the big city, to see an important official about obtaining a permit or license that he needed. The matter was very important to him, and he was most impatient to have it over and done with. So it seemed to him that the railroad train in which he sat, looking out the window, was moving much too slowly. Why could the wheels not turn faster? Unable to contain himself, he stood up, rolled up his sleeves, and began pushing hard on the side of the train, with all his strength. He puffed and heaved, his face grew red, and sweat rolled down his face, as he worked away, pushing and pushing.

"Of course, the passengers around him were curious. 'What in the world are you doing?' they wanted to know. 'Why are you heaving and pushing so hard?' He looked at them: 'What do you mean, why? I know', he said, gasping and puffing to catch his breath, 'that when I push my wagon from behind, out on my farm, it goes faster. Well, I am in a great hurry now to get to the big city. So I am pushing the train to make it go faster.'

"Needless to say, the passengers were not impressed. They laughed at him: 'You are a yokel indeed. Even if you stood behind this train and pushed, it would never mean a thing; and you are certainly ac-complishing nothing when you stand inside the train and shove and heave. This train has a powerful engine that can do all the pulling necessary. Sit down and relax!'

"We have a good God in heaven", the Ḥafetz Ḥayyim continued, "who manages the world with a mighty power that is beyond our understanding. He provides for every kind and species of living creature, from a tiny mite to the largest buffalo. Do you really think for one moment that with all your huffing and puffing, with all the extra work and toil that you put in, including the few hours a week when you should get away from it all and study Torah, you are helping Him in any way to provide you your sustenance? You are inside the world that He sustains, not outside it. Not all your extra exertion of energy can add a thing to the income that Heaven allots you."

56
HE DOES NOT NEED HELP

The Ḥafetz Ḥayyim once used the same illustration to make another point: In his yeshiva (Torah academy) in Radun there was a young adult student who was very learned and reverent toward Heaven. He learned that the Ḥafetz Ḥayyim was quite displeased with those who used a scissors to trim their beard; and from that time on he was most careful never to touch his beard in any way, but to let it grow completely naturally. This gave him, however, an unkempt and slovenly appearance, and as a result he had trouble in finding a girl who would marry him.

Once arrangements for a match were made between his family and the parents of a fine young lady. It was a very good and commendable match in every respect, and both families were pleased. The arrangements were about to be completed to everyone's satisfaction, when the young lady heard that the young man, who was praised to her so highly, sported a wild, untrimmed beard. She refused even to see him. She wanted nothing to do with a bearded man (as full beards were quite out of fashion then).

Thoroughly mortified and downhearted, the young Talmud student returned to the yeshiva and told his friends of his misfortune. Their answer was: "In that case you have no real choice. After all, there is no prohibition at all in religious law against taking a scissors and trimming your beard. But to remain without a wife is very strongly forbidden. You know you have had trouble before on account of your beard, in trying to get married. Now you have to start worrying that you may *never* be able to marry, which is an enormous wrong. Then it is certainly better to give up your strict practice about the beard...."

Perplexed, the young man went to see the Ḥafetz Ḥayyim and told *him* the whole story of the marriage arrangements that were almost settled and then were completely cancelled. And he told him of the many previous difficulties he had encountered in trying to find a wife. Finally he related the advice that his friends among the yeshiva students had given him.

"No", said the Ḥafetz Ḥayyim, "don't you listen to them. Their advice is of no value. Have you ever seen a freight train made up of a long line of railroad cars, laden with all kinds of merchandise? You can find trains consisting of sixty or seventy cars, every one loaded to the top with produce and wares; and one engine pulls them all. Suppose it occurred to someone to help that 'poor little single engine' pull the big, heavy load, by going to the back of the train and pushing. Wouldn't he be an object of scorn and ridicule to everyone who saw him? It is exactly the same here. The blessed Lord arranges matches and marriages. If His job in your case is not so easy (so to speak), do you think you are going to help Him and make it easier by trimming down your beard?"

57

THE TEMPORARY PRISONER

In the Talmud (B'rachoth 8b) it is told: Rabbi Elazar took sick, whereupon Rabbi Yoḥanan came to see him. He asked the sick man, "Do you have any liking for the afflictions?" Rabbi Elazar replied, "Neither for them nor for the reward for them." At that Rabbi Yoḥanan told him, "Give me your hand." He gave him his hand, and he brought him to his feet. He made him well.

Now, a question could be asked about this: If so, if a man can just shake off his afflictions and suffering, and rid himself of them without difficulty, then it should be possible for every person, when he sees afflictions and troubles coming upon him, to step forth and declare, "O Divine Sovereign of the world, I do not want them — neither them nor the reward for them!" Is that true?

It is not true at all. If anyone thinks so, he is sadly mistaken. Let us explain with a parable:

A certain writer of novels and short stories suddenly felt a strong desire to write a novel about the life of prisoners sentenced to spend many years behind bars. What did he do? He went to see the warden of the largest prison in the country, introduced himself, and explained who he was and what he wanted to do. Then he asked permission to spend some time there as a prisoner: He would wear the same clothes, sleep in a cell, and take his meals with them. He would go out with a work-gang of prisoners sentenced to hard labor, and would toil with them. Whatever punishment or deprivation they suffered, he would suffer with them. Above all, he explained, he wanted to be taken for a prisoner. No one but the warden, if possible, should know who he really was.

Since he was a well-known novelist of repute, the warden granted him his request. He was brought in under guard and registered as a prisoner. He was given prison clothes and put in a cell, behind bars, together with seasoned, hardened criminals. With them he went out to the hard labor that they had to do every day. And he had to suffer greatly at their hands, since they always maltreated new prisoners at the beginning. No one suspected that he was anything but a convicted criminal, paying his debt to society.

A few weeks went by, and the novelist began to feel that it was all a bit too much for him. This prison life, he found, was far too harsh for him to bear. He had never imagined it would be as fiercely taxing as this, and he felt his strength starting to give way. If he did not get out soon, his health would surely suffer. Moreover, for writing his novel he had more than enough first-hand knowledge and experience. He would gain no further useful information by staying. He knew thoroughly what a prisoner underwent within those dark grey walls.

Discreetly he sent word to the warden. To everyone's utter surprise, the warden himself came, and ordered this "prisoner" released, after which the two walked off together. Soon enough all the prisoners learned through the prison "grapevine" that their former fellow-inmate had changed into street clothes and left, a perfectly free man, after shaking hands warmly with the warden.

A great murmur of protest welled up within the prison, and it became a shout: "What is this?" the prisoners protested. "What happened here? Is there no justice? Is this fair? He was one of us, a plain common convicted criminal just like the rest of us. He wanted to go free; so he sent for the warden and went out free — just like that. Well, we also want to go free!"

Unable to quiet the prisoners any other way, the warden had them assemble in the mess hall (where they took their meals) and he spoke to them: "Look: this is all a mistake. The man was no criminal. He never committed a serious crime in his life. He was never on trial and was never convicted of any wrongdoing. He is a well-known novelist, and he needed background information about life in prison, so that he can write about it in his next book. At his request I allowed him to stay here as a prisoner and live among you as if he was one of you. Now he decided that he had learned enough — and suffered enough — and he wished to leave. Does anyone here think I should have kept him here, against his will? And now one more question: Does anyone here think that he is also entitled to leave at his request, just because I let the novelist go home?"

There were murmurs of frustration among the seasoned, hardened criminals; but none of them had anything to say.

The moral of the story is obvious: No conclusions should be drawn about other people who are stricken by illness, from the case of Rabbi Elazar.

58
PLEASANT AND UNPLEASANT IMPRISONMENT

There is another way, too, to understand the Talmudic passage cited above, about Rabbi Elazar.

In a certain city the authorities built a new large, imposing prison.

As soon as the structure was finished, they appointed a warden and an administrative staff, with a full crew of sentries and guards. In short, the prison was made "ready for business", and the people who manned it waited for the courts to start sending them inmates.

Yet strange as it seems, a good many weeks went by, and not even one man was convicted of a serious crime, to be sentenced to a prison term. The cells stood empty; the guards went idle.

As the days went by, the warden grew worried: From the country's capital, the national government might decide to send a committee to inspect the prisons; and if they found this one without a single inmate who needed watching, they might decide that the city did not need this prison at all, and the warden and his entire staff, down to the last sentry at the gate, might find themselves without employment.

What did the warden do? He picked himself up and went out into the street, and kept walking till he found a poor vagrant, a wandering soul without two pennies to his name. The warden simply invited him to come and live at the prison, as an inmate. "Listen to me", he said. "In any case, you have nowhere to live, and you don't know where your next meal is coming from. Come and stay with us. Of course, you will wear prison clothes and be registered as an inmate. But you will receive three meals a day and a place to sleep. All you have to do is say that you are there as a convicted criminal, if anyone comes and asks you."

"And what will you pay me for this service?"

"I told you: You will receive three good meals a day and a place to sleep. I can even guarantee you a daily ration of whiskey, and a little pocket-money now and then." The penniless vagrant shrugged his shoulders and accepted. What did he have to lose?

In a few days, however, the "drought" of prisoners was over. There was an outbreak of crimes in the city, and the police caught the culprits. Put on trial and convicted, the offenders were duly brought to the prison and placed in the brand-new cells. The prison was "in business" at last. With no further need for the poor vagrant, the warden gave him a few dollars and sent him off.

After the pleasant stay inside the prison walls, the vagrant found it a bit unsettling to be out on his own again. In a fit of pique he went into a bar and used the few dollars in his pocket (his first real money in years) to get thoroughly drunk. That made him so elated that he went into the street in a belligerent mood and took to attacking every person he met and smashing every shop-window he could reach. Before he quite knew what was happening, he found himself being taken by the police to the prison. "Oh no you don't!" he exclaimed. "I am not going in there unless you promise me three good meals a day, a place to sleep, a daily ration of whiskey, and a little pocket-money — just as it was before."

He kept up his tirade until they reached the prison gates, when the warden came out to see what the disturbance was all about. "You confounded fool!" he shouted at the vagrant, once he grasped the situation. "Quiet down. The first time, you were not guilty of any crime. We needed you here, so we gave you those terms, including whiskey and pocket-money, as long as you would come and stay. Now you are here as a plain hoodlum, on a charge of drunk and disorderly behavior. Just come along quietly."

When Rabbi Elazar became subject to afflictions, he certainly did not receive them because he deserved them, as punishment for wrong-doing, but because he welcomed them for the sake of the great reward that awaits a person who accepts suffering cheerfully, out of his love for the Almighty. For that reason, when his pains became unbearable, he had the right to say, *no more* — neither them nor the reward for them. We, however, are as full of sins as a pomegranate is full of seeds. Our afflictions do not beset us because we want the reward of accepting them out of love for the Almighty. Then what right have we to say we want "neither them nor their reward"?

59
THE REASON FOR THE FREQUENT CALAMITIES

In the recent decades of our history, troubles and calamities have beset our people thick and fast. Before one misfortune ended, the beginning of another was already in sight. Hardly a day has failed to bring more woe than the day before. Over and over, people have asked, "Why all this great fury and anger that Heaven has been displaying toward us?"

The Ḥafetz Ḥayyim once explained it with an illustration:

In the small towns of Lithuania and Poland (as in Israel today) most small grocery stores and little shops sell to their customers on credit for short periods of time. When a term of credit is over, they collect from a customer what he owes, and then give him credit again.

This goes on, though, only as long as a storekeeper has no thought or plan of closing up his shop and going out of business. If, however, some reason arises for the owner to give up the store for good, he stops extending credit. When a customer appears in the store, he explains, "Listen, my friend: As long as I had no thought of closing up permanently, I always sold you anything you wanted on credit, even for fairly long periods. Now I am about to give up the store entirely. I cannot sell any longer on credit, but have to insist on cash."

This is the nature of the reason for all these disasters and calamities that keep befalling us with such frequency. As it were, the blessed Lord is getting ready to close down the store in this world and put it out of business — which means that our righteous Messiah is already standing at the threshold. There is one view among the Sages that in the "ultimate future" of the Messianic era, the mitzvoth will be repealed. So at a time like this, credit can no longer be extended. We can no longer receive forgiveness for sins, Divine protection and sustenance, for the merit of the mitzvoth we will keep later on. The Almighty requires payment at once, on the spot, for every wrongful, sinful deed that we commit. Since we have not returned to Him in complete repentance, we must pay through tribulations; and for this reason the dire troubles beset us with such frequency — to purify us for the advent of our righteous Messiah — speedily, in our day.

60
WITH ALL YOUR HEART

In the early decades of this century a son of the Ḥafetz Ḥayyim, named Abraham, passed away. He had been a brilliant, outstanding Talmud scholar, and while still a young man, had produced many *hiddushim*, original explanations and clarifications in the Talmud (which his father later cited in his *Likkutey Halachoth*).

It was a sad, mournful day when the funeral procession followed the body slowly through the town of Radun out to the Jewish cemetery. There the Ḥafetz Ḥayyim began his *hesped,* his words of praise and lament for the son he had lost. He said (in part):

In the terrible years of persecution and pillage, 1648–49, the Almighty saw fit to pour out His wrath on dozens of holy Jewish communities [in Eastern Europe]. Thousands of Jews were slain and slaughtered in holy martyrdom. Well, in one small village a widow lived with her only son, a lad more precious to her than the apple of her eye. Her little house stood at the edge of the village; and when the accursed hordes of Chmielnitzki came on their rampage, they fell on that little house at once, and slew the widow's only son right before her eyes.

Too thunderstruck to say a word, the woman stood there mute in her grief, her hands held out, palms upward to heaven. Her eyes were dry; the wound was too deep for tears. But she whispered something to the Creator, standing thus before Him:

"Divine Sovereign of the world, in every human being Thou didst implant a heart, to enable him to love Thee. I have always tried to have love for Thee. Every day, morning and evening, I said the *Sh'ma.* I said, *And you shall love the Lord your God with all your heart and with all your soul and with all your might.* Only, sinful servant of Thine that I am, I could not really love Thee with all my heart, because half of it was filled with love for my boy, whom I bore. Now, however, Thy will has been done, and my son has been taken from me. Now I can love Thee with *all* my heart."

All my life (the Ḥafetz Ḥayyim continued) I wished to love the Lord with all my heart. Yet I am only a creature of flesh and blood, and I am the father of sons. It is only human nature for a father to have compassion and love for his children. Willingly or not, I divided my heart into segments, giving a part to each of my children. Now that the Almighty has seen fit to take one of them from me, I am left with another section of my heart, with which to love Him. . . ."

61

THE FILTHY JEWELS

In our morning prayers we ask, "... and unify our heart to love and revere Thy name"; in other words, let our heart be filled with but one particular love — for the blessed Lord. For we know well that a man's heart is generally filled with many loves and affections: for his father and mother, for his wife and children ... and his love can even go in directions that do not please the Almighty at all — to objects of desire and craving. All these affections and loves can mingle with one's love for the blessed Lord.

It can be understood the better with a parable:

A rich man once found it necessary to set out on a long journey. He called one of his servants to him, who always attended faithfully to his wishes, and he told him, "I have to leave tomorrow morning on a long trip, and will be away quite a while. I am leaving you in charge of my house and property, knowing that I can rely on you to watch over everything properly. Mainly, though, there is one most important thing that I ask of you: One room is especially precious to me, and I want you to take particular care of it. Promise me that you will watch over it constantly and guard it above all else."

The servant promised to watch over it faithfully, and the rich man set off on his trip. With his employer gone, though, the servant became curious to see what was in that room. He wanted to know what made it so precious that the owner wanted it guarded so well. He unlocked the door, went in, and searched long and thoroughly — till he found some locked chests. Rummaging among the collection of keys that the owner left him, he soon found the right ones and opened them. And he feasted his eyes on a veritable fortune in gold and precious jewels, whose like he had never seen in his life. Now he understood, of course, why his employer had insisted that he guard the room so well.

He stood there spellbound, gazing at the gold and precious stones, till at last the surprise and the spell wore off. Then he noticed to his amazement that these precious wares lay in mud and filth. Except for those on the surface it was even hard to see how really superb and valuable the contents were.

"What a peculiar employer I have," thought the servant. "Here he comes and orders me to watch this room almost with my life — because he keeps these treasures in it; and he himself lets them stay in this muck and filth!"

Arrived in the world of truth after his death, a man must stand before Heaven's court of justice and have all the limbs and parts of his body carefully inspected, to see if they were used in purity and holiness, and if no sin was done with them. Now, there is no need to add that the most important inspection is made of the heart.

Well, what do you think the heavenly court of justice ought to find in a man's heart? — a pure and true love for the blessed Creator. That is akin to a precious treasure. In fact, not all the gold and silver in the world can equal it.

For our numerous sins, though, what does the heavenly court find in a man's heart? — muck and mire, dirt and filth, and everything disgusting. The very thought of finding such contents together with the love of God is utterly unbearable. Try to imagine then the shame that will suffuse a person's face at that moment, before the heavenly tribunal.

For this reason we ask every day in our morning prayers, "unify our heart to love and revere Thy name": We beseech, "O Sovereign of the world, make our love for Thee be one and only, singular and unique in our heart. Let no room be left in it for any other love but this!"

62
THE POWER BEHIND THE THRONE

If you are ever in a railroad station, either on board a train or on the platform, you will notice that shortly before the train is to leave the station, the conductor sounds a loud toot or whistle. It is the first signal that the train is about to depart; and many people come hurrying at once to take their places in the train. Others, on the other hand, show no hurry until they hear the second signal. When the third whistle sounds, however, every passenger must be on board, because the train will not wait for anyone, be he the most important and distinguished personage. And it is the same story at every single station on the way where the railroad train stops.

Ordinary, simple people who do not give the matter any great thought imagine that this conductor who blows the whistle is the commander or captain of the train: it goes and stops at his order, and he decides the time of every departure and arrival. Knowledgeable people know, however, that the man who sounds the whistle is only an employee who does not rank high among the officials of the railway system. The man who really decides all the details about the journey of the train sits far away, probably in the capital city. He gives his orders to the officials under him, and they pass them on to the employees under them, till finally the man who sounds the whistle receives his particular instructions.

It is the same in the regulation of this world. We look at a mortal king of flesh and blood, and we see him wielding sovereign power. He has supreme authority over everything in an entire large country. The country, however, may be only part of an empire, ruled by an emperor who thus is the monarch over many countries. There were even "cosmocrats", mighty emperors who ruled the entire known world of their time, from end to end.

Many mistakenly think that such a king or mighty ruler really wields power, and the regulation and control of a part of the world is truly in his hands while he sits on the throne — as though it is the sun that has dominion with its light by day, and the moon reigns at night.

What absolute fools they are. Don't they know that this dominion has a true Sovereign, and it is He who sets kings on their thrones and grants rulers their power? It is the blessed Creator who sends the sun shining on the earth by day and casts darkness at night. And in His hand (His power) He holds the hearts of kings and rulers. Dominion is His to give or to withdraw, as He pleases.

The mightiest ruler is only His servant, carrying out His wishes.

63

WHY THE WORLD MAKES NO SENSE

A traveling man once had to spend a Sabbath in a village. Saturday morning he went to the synagogue for the prayer-service. When it came time for the reading of the Torah, the man saw that the *gabbai* (the head of the congregation) called people to the Torah according to no sort of order or system. For the first *aliyah* he called a distinguished *kohen* who sat up front. For the next *aliyah* he called a Levite who sat at the other end of the synagogue. The third man he called was at a different corner, in the southeast part. And thus he kept jumping around in his choice of people to call up.

After the prayer-service, the traveler went over to the *gabbai*. "Please forgive me", he said, "that I, just a traveler passing through, dare to speak to you like this. It is just that I could not help wondering at the peculiar, random way in which you selected the people to call to the Torah. After all, you have the same people at the prayer-service every week. In my synagogue it is likewise a fixed, unchanging congregation; and so we work with a definite system: Every week the worshippers in a certain part of the synagogue are called up, and so it goes in a set order. You seem to work in utter confusion, with no system at all!"

"That", said the *gabbai,* "is not true. Forgive me, but you are mistaken. We have a system and method of our own. Since you are here only for one Sabbath, you find it puzzling. If you stayed here a while, you would realize that one *kohen* is called first to the Torah this week because a different *kohen* was called last week; and the same applies to those called up afterward. It all works out quite well."

There are many people like that traveling man. They puzzle and wonder at the arrangement they find in the world, that seems so strange to them: Superior people live abased and lowly, and inferior and unworthy people are exalted in rank. A righteous man of piety has a difficult life, and a wicked man lives well. People find these and similar matters perplexing, not to be understood.

They have to realize, however, that they are only like itinerant travelers in this world, stopping over for a night. All their days on earth are like a passing shadow. In such a short time how can they possibly understand adequately the way of the regulation of the world?

64

THE HOLY ONE IS MORE GENEROUS

One day an esteemed and respected wealthy Jew named Reuven received a visit from some friends, accompanied by a matchmaker, who suggested that he would do well to consider forming a marital bond with another wealthy Jew, named Shimon. One had a son and the other a daughter, and the matchmaker believed the two would make a fine couple. Shimon too, said the matchmaker (and the friends assented) was a worthy man of distinction.

The two men of wealth duly met and discussed the matter, and they agreed that on the first of April (a few months away) each of them was to give ten thousand dollars to a third party, known to them both, who would hold the money in trust as a dowry for the couple; and then the *t'na'im*, the formal terms of the marriage arrangement, would be written, making the engagement of the couple official.

When the first of April came, Reuven sent word to Shimon that it was time for each to pay his share of the dowry. The reply came from Shimon that it was indeed so, but he had been unable to prepare the full amount, and he therefore asked for a delay till the first of July. Reuven thought it over, and agreed.

When the first of July came, Reuven again sent a messenger to Shimon with a written note, to remind him that the time had come to provide the money for the dowry. Once more, however, Shimon wrote back that he had been unable to gather the full amount he needed; and he therefore asked for another extension of time — till the first of November. Yet, he added, even by that date he probably would not have all the money he needed, but only half. The other half he could provide by some later date.

Once more Reuven thought it over, and once more he agreed, because by nature he was easy-going and generous. He waited patiently till the first of November, then sent Shimon a reminder by messenger, as before, that the money was due. This time the reply was that he,

Shimon, had no money at all. If, however, Reuven was willing to go ahead with the marriage arrangements, without requiring Shimon's share of the dowry, he was prepared to consent and the young couple could become engaged.

This, however, Reuven was not prepared to accept. He terminated the negotiations with Shimon and made the same arrangements, instead, with a wealthy Jew named Levi. On a bright and sunny day their grown children were married to one another.

In about a year an infant son was born to the couple, whereupon Reuven sent the *shammash,* the caretaker of the local synagogue, to tell all his relatives and friends that their presence would be welcome at the ceremony of circumcision. Likewise, said Reuven, the *shammash* was to bring the message to the relatives of Levi. At that the *shammash* asked, "Shall I also go and tell Shimon? After all, he almost became related to you as Levi did."

"No", said Reuven. "If I wanted to invite all the people to whom I could have become related through the marriage, there would be no end to it. I am a wealthy man, you know, and many people always want to form marital ties with a rich family."

"True", said the *shammash,* "yet Shimon's case is different, you know. Others just wanted to marry a child of theirs to one of your children. Shimon, however, made definite arrangements and terms with you. The whole thing was cancelled only because of money matters." Nevertheless, Reuven refused to change his mind. He would welcome to the celebration only his actual relatives, and not those who wished to be or almost became related to him, and only failed to do so on account of circumstances.

For a respectable, worthy man of conduct above reproach, this was an understandable attitude. The blessed Creator, however, does not give such an answer. If a man wants to do a mitzvah, a religious good deed — which means that he wants to draw close and become attached to Him — but through circumstances beyond his control he cannot manage to do it, the Holy One, blessed is He, does not see him as some unrelated stranger who has never formed any kind of bond or link with Him, but rather like an actual close relative, like true kin. Scripture considers him as though he is already closely linked to Him, because he wished to do a mitzvah.

With this in mind we can understand Scripture's words, *let the heart of those who seek the Lord rejoice* (Psalms 105:3). At first sight it seems puzzling why Scripture should have chosen the expression "those who seek". It means to convey, however, that even those who still only seek the Lord, trying to do one of His mitzvoth because He ordered it done, but they haven't done it yet because various circumstances have prevented them, so that they remain in the state of "seekers" and no more — even their heart will nevertheless rejoice. For the Holy One accepts with affection both them and their attempt to draw close; and He regards them as though already closely linked to him, as relatives and kin, as it were.

65

TO ACHIEVE A HEALTHY LIFE OF DEVOTION

A devout Jew works and strives to serve the Almighty, each according to his strength and ability. Still, we have our ups and downs. We cannot remain always on the same level in the worship of the Lord. Sometimes we may become negligent and indolent, and then we can descend to the level of sinners; and then we make a concerted effort and rouse ourselves to diligence in worshipping Him, till we succeed in returning to Him in penitence.

We have to bear in mind, though, that the Almighty's wish is that we should not be satisfied with serving and worshipping Him intermittently, today using good sense and doing well, and tomorrow causing some sin to occur (Heaven forbid). He rather wants our heart devoted constantly to the Holy One: that we should serve Him whole-heartedly and willingly always.

We could compare our condition to that of a sick man whose friend met him in the street. "How are you?" his friend asked him. "Not well", he replied. "You should not know what I feel. I am sick."

"What kind of illness do you have?"

"I suffer from fever."

His friend looked at him closely. "To tell you the truth", he said, "you do not look sick at all."

"Well, in a way you are right. Today I really feel all right. I have no high temperature at all."

"Then why are you looking so worried and distressed? You have gotten better!"

"Oh, you just don't know the kind of sickness I have. The nature of my fever is that one day my temperature may go up alarmingly, and then I am confined to bed with pains. Tomorrow the temperature may go down, and I can walk around as well as anyone. And so it has been going on for weeks now. Then even today, when my temperature is normal, I am still a sick man."

This is our condition at present. True, there are days when, spiritually speaking, we are completely healthy. We serve the Almighty with all our heart. The illness shows up in us, however, when we suddenly grow careless and indolent and just slide back into our foolish ways. So the illness rages in our system even in those days when we serve the Almighty and worship Him properly. It is merely lying dormant then, waiting for its next chance to flare up.

This is why the Almighty demands of us, *that their children ... may hear and learn to fear the Lord your God all the days* (Deuteronomy 31:13) — not intermittently, sometimes yes and sometimes no, being one way today and quite different tomorrow, but we should rather worship the Lord "all the days" whole-heartedly.

66
GRAB WHAT YOU CAN

Sometimes a Jew may stand and pray to the Sovereign Master of the world, and he may yet feel that his heart is void and empty. He cannot concentrate and infuse his prayer with content. Then the Jew may fall into grief and despair. He may wish to cry out, "Enough! Since I have been unable to focus my heart, there is no point in continuing to pray. What worth or value can prayer have without any focus on its meaning?"

This, however, is a mistaken approach. Let us explain the mattei with a parable:

A little girl once stood at her mother's vegetable stand, selling the various kinds of produce. Along came a drunkard who began snatching the vegetables from the stand. At that the bewildered child began to cry and weep bitterly, not knowing what to do. A wise man came along and said, "You silly girl, why are you standing and crying? Some of the vegetables are still left. Seize them quickly and run! If you don't, you will not have even these left."

Even if the Jew we have described can manage to say a small part of his prayers with the proper focus of the heart, he must hurry and "grab"; otherwise he will not have even this little bit. When he cannot concentrate in the synagogue, it is no time to give up in despair. Let him get what he can!

67
THE WASTED REQUEST

If we consider the matter honestly, we will find that our main concern and concentration in our prayer is when we come to physical, worldly affairs, connected with food, earning a living, and so on. There we shed tears and concentrate our heart on true, earnest entreaty. When it comes, however, to prayer about other matters, such as repentance, proper knowledge and understanding, achieving a love of the Torah — spiritual matters — then only a select, precious few pour out their entreaty from the depth of their heart, with tears and lament.

How well we can be compared to a certain brainless soldier:

A king once came to inspect a military camp in his country. The soldiers stood at attention, formed in their ranks, while the king moved about examining them carefully. Needless to say, everyone strove to the utmost to look his best and make a good impression; and the king was pleased at the fine sight they made. Said he:

"You all look very good to me, and I am pleased indeed at what I have seen of you. Therefore I grant every one of you the right to come forward and ask any favor you wish, within reason, and it will be granted."

At that one soldier sprang forward: "Your majesty, I have something to request."

"Yes?" said the king. "What is your request?"

"I wish your majesty to order that my daily rations of food are to be given me regularly, every day without fail."

Back in the barracks his fellow-soldiers poured out their scorn and contempt on his head: "You perfect idiot! For this you had to go and trouble the king with a special request? As long as you do your army duty faithfully and they keep you in the armed forces, you get your meals regularly in any case, automatically. You even get clothing and anything else you need. The king's treasury pays for it, for every soldier in the army. What lunacy it is to go and ask the king for regular meals, when he was in a particularly cheerful mood, ready to grant us special favors."

That is exactly what we are like. We do not understand that the main theme of our entreaty has to be the ability to become good devout, observant Jews. We must pray and implore Heaven's help to be able to be loyal soldiers, serving our blessed Maker in love and devotion. Then we will automatically be entitled to receive our "rations" of daily food, our clothing and all our needs — out of the "royal treasury" of Divine providence, as "regulars" in the "service" of the supreme King of kings, the Holy One, blessed is He.

68
THE REPEATED MEANINGLESS PLEA

A poor man in very pressing circumstances once met someone on the street who was known as one of the well-to-do people in the city. "Excuse me, sir", said the indigent man. "I have a great favor to ask of you: Could you grant me the kindness of lending me a thousand dollars? I have come down badly in the world, but now a chance has come up to go into a small business venture. If you do me this favor, you will be saving my family and me from starvation or the poorhouse."

"Very well", said the wealthy man. "You look like a man of integrity. At the moment, however, I don't have that much money with me; and besides, I am in a great hurry. So do *me* a favor and come to my house at five o'clock this evening. Then I will gladly lend you the money."

Remembering his promise, the rich man made it his business to be home by five, and he waited for his expected visitor. He waited till half past five, then till six — and the needy person never came. Well, thought the wealthy man, something might have happened to the poor fellow that kept him from coming.

The next day the wealthy man was again walking on the street, when he again encountered the indigent man. Once more this poor person started asking him for help: "You see, sir, I now have a good chance to go into a fine little business venture, and financially I am in very great trouble. If you could only let me have a thousand dollars for a while, it would really save my life."

"I told you yesterday", said the rich man, "to come to my house, and I would let you have the money. I even waited for you a whole hour — and you never came. Never mind, though. What is past is past. If you wish, come to my house *this* evening at five, and the money will be waiting for you."

Again the wealthy man arranged his schedule and curtailed his other activities, so as to be home by the appointed hour of five. Again he waited — and again the indigent man never appeared.

The third day, sure enough, the two met once more in the street; and sure enough, the poor man began his old refrain all over again: He had a chance to go into business, his financial situation was dreadful, he needed a loan of a thousand dollars, and so forth.

The wealthy man could no longer contain himself. "You had better stop bothering me", he burst out. "I see there is not a word of truth in what you are telling me. You don't need any money. If you really needed it you would have come to me yesterday or the day before, at the time I told you, when I was waiting for you at home; and you would have gotten the money I prepared for you. I don't know what your game is; maybe you are some kind of a crank; but you say words with your mouth that you do not mean with your heart.". . .

Every morning we pray, "... be Thou gracious to us and teach us. ... Give our heart the power to understand and discern, to hearken and learn ... Enlighten our eyes in Thy Torah, and bind our heart to Thy mitzvoth. ... Grace us with Thy gift of knowledge, understanding and insight"; and so we plead in many supplications and prayers.

Most certainly the blessed Lord is ready graciously to bestow on us wisdom, understanding and insight. He is prepared to give us a heart with which to comprehend His holy Torah. From His end, as it were, there is never any restraint or refusal. On the contrary, He helps any-one who does a mitzvah, and is ready to bestow His beneficent aid upon him, as he but asks.

For this, though, He asks but one thing of us: to come to Him in His home, which means in the *beth midrash,* the house of study, to have set hours for Torah study there.

For our many sins, though, those supplications and pleas in our morning prayer are nothing more than lip service: pretty phrases that we mouth. When we pray and talk with Him, we implore Him to lend us His thousand dollars, so to speak. When we leave the synagogue and go on our way, we sink head and shoulders into the vapid trivia of this world, and we forget completely what we begged for.

Tomorrow we return blithely, as if nothing happened, and we be-seech His aid again; and then, just as soon, we go and forget that too.

This is why the prophet says, *Take words with you* (Hosea 14:3): Take with you those words that you spoke. Do not forget them, but rather keep well in mind those words of supplication with which you entreated Him. Then *return to the Lord* (*ibid.*): then your return to Him in penitence can be complete and whole-hearted.

69
OUR AVAILABLE CASH

Consider a man of means who lives in comfort and ease, dwelling in a large, expansive house with many rooms, furnished in splendor and luxury, with cooks and chefs who prepare the finest foods for him, and a staff of servants to wait on him hand and foot and carry out his every wish. When a man like that has to go on a long trip sometimes, to a far destination, he is not concerned at all about managing on the road: where he will find comfortable, well-furnished rooms to stay; where he will obtain good food for his meals; how he will get servants to attend upon him. He has no such worry or concern because he knows well that to deal with all these questions he needs to do only one thing: take along enough money. For money you get fine rooms in the best quality hotels, splendid meals in superb restaurants, and even servants and attendants ready to do your every bidding.

Thus for all such problems the key to the answer is money.

Well, it really is the same with us:

When the holy Temple stood in ancient Jerusalem — the house of God, functioning in perfect order, we thus had a place where we could obtain all we needed. A man came and brought an animal offering, and his sin was atoned and forgiven; or he brought a *sh'lamim*, a peace-offering, and he prayed to the good Lord to bestow blessing on the work of his hands; and He (be He blessed) manifested Himself to us constantly, He was always there, in our need and entreaty. For the power of animal offerings in the Sanctuary was great indeed.

Now, however, we are forever wandering and traveling on the roads of exile. So now we always need to have at least a little "ready cash" with us, at hand — which means Torah study and prayer. Thus it says, *so we will pay for bullocks with our lips* (Hosea 14:3). If we study about offerings in the course of our prayer, it is as though we have brought an offering at the Temple. This, then, is our "money purse", with which even a man tossing about on the roads of exile can attain all the good spiritual things that he needs. Even if he is not "in his own house" — at his Sanctuary of old — his "money" of Torah study and prayer will stand him in good stead to let him get whatever his heart wishes.

70

TO NEGLECT OR CURE THE ILLNESS

There are irreligious Jews who, truth to tell, have not yet drawn very far away from the path of the Torah. Deep in their heart the spark of authentic Jewish faith still burns bright. Left to themselves, they might possibly continue conducting themselves as observant, praise-worthy Jews. The trouble is that they see how others act — completely unrestrained and undisciplined; and they crave to be like the others. So they are led astray to follow them; they are drawn into the company of the others, until they sink completely into the abyss of sin.

It can be illustrated by a parable:

In a certain village an epidemic broke out (may Heaven spare us), and almost all the inhabitants there fell sick with the swiftly spreading mortal disease. The physicians in the village knew of no cure for it, and in fact did not even know its cause.

However, one of the people who fell sick heard that in a neigh-boring city there was a very learned and famous doctor who was an expert specifically in this disease: He had already cured thousands of it, literally saving their lives. This villager sent for one of his good friends at once, and he implored him, "I beg you, do me a favor: Don't spare any effort or expense, but ride as swiftly as you can to the city, and bring that doctor here. Please do everything you can to make sure you get the doctor to come here ... because I don't want to die!"

"Why are you so impatient and impulsive," asked his friend, "more than everyone else in the village? You are not the only one with this disease. Almost everyone here has it. Then why don't you wait till you talk things over with the other sick people in the village, and all of you together can invite the physician to come and cure the whole lot of you? And besides, how do you know for certain that this doctor really knows how to cure this dread illness? Even the greatest physician cannot be certain that he will succeed in a particular case. Then is it really worth going to so much trouble?"

The sick man grew angry at his friend: "Look here. In this place no one knows any cure for the illness. Do you want me just to sit and wait until all the others think it over and decide to call that famous physician? Why should I care in the least what they do, when my life is in danger? I have to do everything I can to save myself. ... Now, you say I cannot be certain that he will really succeed in finding a cure for my ailment. That too is nonsense. When a man's life is in danger, he has to do everything he can to save himself, even if there is not very much hope."

How well this applies to the people mentioned above. If they only knew how mortally sick they are, they would certainly pay no attention to what others are doing, but would send out an emergency call immediately for the expert physician. From him they would get the effective medicine called repentance and would achieve a cure for their ailment without running with the pack of those mortally sick people who feel and sense nothing and have never a care about themselves.

Just think the matter over: With an illness of the body, which is only a temporary concern — because a person has his body for only seventy or eighty-odd years at best — a sensible person does everything he can to save himself. He goes to doctors even if he is not altogether sure of them. He takes their advice even if he is not certain how good it is. Then where a serious illness befalls a person's life-spirit, which is something enduring, that lives both in this world and the next, how much more must he do everything possible to save himself — to pull free from the bonds of sin — without paying the slightest attention to what anyone else is doing.

71
THE CLAIM TO PAID WAGES

How many sensitive pious Jews have complained in anguish, and go on complaining, their mouths filled with arguments and contentions against the Almighty, so to speak, over the bitter exile that we have been suffering for over 1900 years. Our fathers and forefathers, generations without end, have been afflicted with every kind of tribulation and calamity in this bitter Diaspora. We have been racked by the severity of our persecution. And we go on suffering and enduring dire troubles and woeful turns of fate. As a result we have become certain that the time has already come to find relief and surcease. It is high time, we insist, for the Almighty to rescue us and send us the righteous Messiah.

Yet if we talk in this vein, we are making nothing but a big mistake.

We have a right to complain about no one but ourselves. We alone are to blame for this pitiful situation.

It can be explained with a parable:

For years a man served faithfully as a clerk and secretary in his employer's place of business. He worked with honesty and integrity, giving full value for his money; and in return, his employer, a wealthy merchant, paid him a good salary week after week, month after month.

The time came when the faithful employee passed away, and the merchant hired his son to take his place. The son did his work with the same loyalty and devotion; but illness carried him off a short while afterward. He left a grown son behind him, however, and the merchant now hired this young man in turn, at the same handsome salary that he had paid the young man's grandfather and father.

A few weeks went by, and one day this new clerk and secretary came into his employer's office to speak to the merchant. "Sir", he said, "I want you to listen to me. I know that my grandfather and my father served you faithfully for a period of forty years altogether; and now I have been working for you for a few weeks. So I have come to demand all the wages that my grandfather and my father earned during those forty years. By my reckoning they earned a total of about 200,000 dollars."

The merchant looked at him and burst out laughing: "What sort of a blessed fool are you? It is true enough that your father and grandfather worked for me for a total of forty years, and they gave me excellent service. But I paid them a regular salary for their work. How can you be so stupid as to think that they worked for me all those years for nothing? How do you think they lived all those years, and provided for their families, if not out of the wages I paid them? And if you have any doubt that I am telling you the truth, I am prepared to show you the ledgers. You will find their signatures for every payment of wages that they received from me."

We come before the blessed Lord and demand that He send us the Messiah, the righteous redeemer; why? — in reward for all the pain and trouble that our fathers and forefathers suffered in the Diaspora;

because they bore it all and continued serving Him and keeping His mitzvoth.

We forget, however, that they received reward and compensation for it: a small recompense in this world, and an immense reward that they continue receiving in the Hereafter, the world-to-come. Then how can we come and demand the compensation that they deserve? We may ask only the very little bit of reward that we have earned by our religious observance and devotion in our time. And we certainly have no right to protest or complain against the blessed Lord (perish the thought). On the contrary, we have to pour out our prayer and supplication to Him, to be able to return to Him in utter repentance. Then He will return to us in His compassion and grace, and He will send us the righteous redeemer — speedily, in our days.

72

A LITTLE AT A TIME

A man who owned a small general store (an emporium) in a little village took a trip to the city to buy the merchandise he needed to refill his emptying shelves. He went to the wholesale merchant with whom he always dealt, and gave him the order for all the items he wanted. "Do me a favor, though", he asked the wholesaler. "Let me have everything on credit for the time being. I don't have any money with me now. As soon as I return home, I will send you the payment in full."

"I am sorry", said the wholesale merchant, "but I cannot extend you any credit now. I have been examining my accounts, and I find that you took merchandise from me several times in the past on credit; and you always promised to pay the bill as soon as you returned home — and you never kept your promises. Can you tell me why I should believe you now?"

At that the village storekeeper began to weep and plead with him: "I beg you to believe me. I was not at fault all those times when I didn't do as I promised, and did not pay my bills." He then went on to explain what had happened each time in the past to prevent him from paying what he owed — each time some different event or set of circumstances. Thus he had always been a victim of circumstances, and was not to blame. "Now, however", he added, "I give you my word of honor that as soon as I get home I will send you the whole amount that I owe you."

He went on pleading and beseeching the wholesaler to have pity on him and his family: because if he received no new merchandise, he would most likely have to close the store and go out of business; and then his family and he would be simply left to starve. . . .

The soft-hearted wholesaler could not remain firm in the face of all the tears and entreaties, and at last he let the village storekeeper have what he wanted. As soon as he went to the back, however, to tell his workers to fill the man's order, his workers all began arguing with him, telling him how absolutely wrong he was to give that man any more goods on credit. "We know that man", they shouted, "and we know what he is like. You will never see a penny of what he owes you. He will simply take home all these items that he needs now, and he will find another excuse why he is not able to pay you anything, and of course it isn't his fault, but please don't make his family starve to death, and so on and so forth. We tell you flatly: you are making a mistake; and we won't lift a finger to bring him any merchandise or wrap it for him!"

At the counter in the front, the village storekeeper stood and heard every word of the argument going on within. As he stood listening, another storekeeper came in, to buy what he needed, and he too stood and listened. It did not take him long to understand the situation; and then he turned to the villager and said, "Let me give you some good advice, that will satisfy both sides to this argument. From what I hear, you want to take a large supply of merchandise now, that will last you for many months. Why do you have to buy so much all at once, so that you will be left owing this wholesale merchant a large sum of money all at once — which evidently you won't be able to pay immediately, in spite of what you promise — and this in addition to what you owe him from the past? Would it not be much better for you to take a small amount of goods, so that you can pay for it right away out of your cash reserves, and even start paying off a bit of your debt from before? I know this man is a wholesaler, and usually he sells only in large quantities. But he wants to help you, and he wants to collect what you owe him from before. So I am certain that he will make an exception in your case and sell you small quantities. When you sell out this merchandise, come back and buy small quantities again, and so again and again, till you straighten out your account with the man here."

This was sound advice indeed, to which both the village storekeeper and the wholesale merchant (and his workers) agreed. The villager bought only as much as he could pay for out of the money that he had brought with him. He took his merchandise home, and when that was sold he came back and bought again a small amount of goods for cash. This practice he continued until, with his slowly accumulating profits, the day came when he could put his business operations on a sound footing.

In our prayers we beseech the blessed Almighty to have compassion and pity on us and send us the Messiah, the righteous redeemer, swiftly in our days. We groan that we cannot bear the suffering any more. The wearying burden of the exile is too much for us. If He will not arise and rescue us in His mercy, we plead, we will surely perish (Heaven forbid) in our anguish.

The blessed Creator is certainly ready and willing to accede to our prayer and grant our petition: for we promise Him in one supplication after another to return to Him in complete repentance. Yet it is only too well known to Him that in spite of all our promises and assurances, we will go back to our "business as usual" and will sin again. Nevertheless, the fact is that He is compassionate and benevolent, and He cannot turn a deaf ear (so to speak) to all our prayer and entreaty and send us away empty-handed. Quite possibly He would yield to our pleas finally, and really send us the righteous redeemer to pull us out of the spiritual dungeon of our exile. The quality of stern justice enters the scene, however (if we may so speak), and holds Him back, arguing that we are *children in whom there can be no trust* (Deuteronomy 32:20). Just look, says this quality: They promise and promise to return in complete redemption; but they have never yet kept their word. How can they be believed now?

So there is no other way for us to take but the approach of that village storekeeper. If it is beyond our means to buy a large quantity of Heaven's goods — the full Messianic redemption — and pay for it with a full return to Him in penitence, is it not better for us to buy in small quantities and pay at once for our purchases? Let us begin turning back to Him in repentance over the small, easy sins we commit: the evil gossip, lies and slanders that we tell. Bit by bit let us pay off our debt of guilt, until we can stand on our own two feet as respectable members of His people, whose word He can trust!

73
"MY POCKETS DID JINGLE"

To whom can we be compared? — to a certain drunken peasant with a purse full of copper pennies in his pocket. Off he went into town, jingling the pennies in his pocket gaily, feeling for all the world as rich as Croesus. He entered a bar, clinking the pennies more loudly than ever; and putting on what he thought was the manner of a Rothschild, he ordered: "Give me a double whiskey from that bottle over there, my good man... and leave the bottle here." When the bottle was empty, its entire contents having drained out of it and into him, he paid out of his vast supply of pennies, and promptly ordered another bottle. If one was good, two of them must certainly be better, he thought. He could still hear the pennies clinking and jingling in his pocket, and so was certain that he was still as rich as Croesus. In his drunken state it never occurred to him to make any kind of calculation to see how much money he actually had and how fast he was spending it.

He kept emptying bottle after bottle, getting more and more drunk, as the supply of pennies in his purse kept dwindling. Thus he spent the night, until morning came and he staggered out of the bar with only a few pennies left in his purse. Few as they were, though, he could still make them clink, and so he waltzed and weaved his way down the street with snatches of song and shouts, as befit his state of intoxication. Of course, whoever saw him just laughed at him in scorn and contempt.

Well, isn't this how *we* behave? In our twenties we have, if you will, a "purse full of copper pennies". It seems to us that the whole world is before us. We have a wealth of knowledge and ability, many years of life lie ahead, and we snatch at the pleasures of this world whereever and however we can. We seize and take and enjoy, without any account of the expense as compared with our resources.

Just like that guzzling drunkard, we are bent on our pursuit of the vain, vapid matters of nonsense in this world, never realizing that the "pennies in our purse" are dwindling away. We reach 25, and soon enough we are 30. In a little while we will be 35 — half our life over, the purse of coins half empty. And still we go dancing and cavorting through the pleasure-halls of life, jingling gaily the copper pennies left in our pocket.

So we go on, getting older. We reach forty, fifty, even sixty; and still we clink loudly the few pennies left us, as though they were a fortune, as though the whole world were still before us. Then we are quite old, in advanced age; only a few years of life are left us; and still we "drink ourselves into intoxication" and pay no mind to the fact that the day is drawing close when our purse will be completely empty: We will leave this life and be called to Heaven's court of justice to give a full account of all we did. . . .

74
THE DIFFERENCE BETWEEN REMEMBERING AND FORGETTING

Reuven lent Shimon a thousand dollars, for an indefinite period. Some time later the two met in the street, and Reuven asked Shimon, "Do you remember that you still owe me a thousand dollars?"

"Do you imagine", Shimon replied, "that I have forgotten something as important and serious as that? You can be sure that from the time I took your money I have not put the matter out of my mind for a moment. The loan is recorded in my account book, and I look forward to the day when, with God's help, I can pay it back in gratitude."

This answer put Reuven's mind at rest. He knew he could depend on Shimon to repay the loan in full. Beyond any doubt Shimon was a man of integrity, who would keep his word.

Suppose, however, that meeting Shimon in the street and reminding him of the loan, Reuven had received a far different answer. Suppose Shimon said that he had no record of such a loan in his account-book, and frankly, he did not remember that he owed Reuven anything... and for all he knew perhaps there had never been such a loan. Then Shimon would have shown himself to be no better than a scoundrel or a swindler. Reuven could reckon that he had probably poured his money down the drain: he would never see it again. If Shimon never took the trouble to make a record of the loan, evidently he cared little about other people's money, and he would never take any particular trouble to repay it.

If a wise man who reveres the word of God happens to have committed a sin, he is filled with remorse over it and turns back at once in complete repentance; and he makes a record of it in his account-book — which means that he wholeheartedly resolves never to forget that he came to grief with this sin, so that he will always keep alert to remain in repentance over it. As King David said, *my sin is ever before me* (Psalms 51:5). As long as he keeps this attitude, we can be sure that he will remain in penitence his entire life.

What, however, if a man who commits a sin gives it no thought and does not turn back at once in contrition and penitence? Then he will never succeed in achieving a proper repentance, because in the course of time he will forget that he sinned once and will simply go on sinning, so that all his life he will remain guilt-laden (Heaven spare us).

This is why the Talmud (tractate Shabbath 12) relates that R. Ishmael decided to study Torah on a Friday night by the light of an oil lamp, certain that he would not absent-mindedly tilt the lamp to give him a better light (which is forbidden on the Sabbath); and in the end he did forget himself while absorbed in his study, and he did tilt the lamp. After the Sabbath, says the Talmud, he wrote in his account-book, "I, Ishmael the son of Elisha, was studying and I tilted the lamp on the Sabbath. When the holy Temple will be rebuilt I will bring a plump sin-offering."

This means that R. Ishmael kept his sin in mind constantly, and all his life he was contrite and concerned about it, worrying that perhaps he had not acquitted himself of his obligation over it. As a result, he spent all his days in complete repentance.

75

OUR PRIVILEGE AND OUR RESPONSIBILITY

When a king goes out on a tour of his country, it is the general custom that a retinue of distinguished officers and noblemen accompanies him from the capital to the first major city that he reaches on his trip. When he arrives there, he is met by a delegation of city notables headed by the mayor. As he leaves the city, this delegation joins his retinue and accompanies him to the next city. Thus he continues from city to town to village, being met everywhere by the heads and notables, come to pay him honor.

Now, a village mayor is not a particularly important officer. As a rule, it is an honor for him to be received by a city mayor. And needless to say, it is difficult for him to obtain an appointment with the governor of a district. As for getting to see the king himself, in the royal palace, he would hardly even think it possible.

Nevertheless, when the king goes on his royal tour through the country, even a lowly minor official like a village mayor has the privilege to be among those who welcome the royal ruler and pay him honor. It becomes his duty to make certain that the people in the village receive their monarch properly, and that the king should find the place made spick and span for his honor, and so forth. Afterward he has to give a full account of all his activities to his superior officers.

In these later generations, that grow spiritually ever weaker, we too come to resemble those village heads.

In the very early generations, the Almighty was accompanied by a retinue of most distinguished personages: the Patriarchs, Moses and Aaron, and the seventy elders. Then came the prophets, the men of the Great Assembly, the early and later Sages of the Talmud, and other consummate Torah scholars. Afterward the generations grew more and more diminished; the level of distinction became ever lower, until the time has come when we, the "village elders", become responsible for the honor of Heaven.

Most certainly we have to remember who and what we really are in comparison with those distinguished officers and noblemen of the Almighty. They towered far above us spiritually. Nevertheless, that does not free us from the heavy obligation and responsibility that lies upon us. We have to be most careful and concerned about the Almighty's honor — for afterward we shall have to give a full and strict account of our activity, to show if we knew how to accord proper respect to the supreme King of kings, the Holy One, blessed is He.

76
WITH THE BEST DEFENSE ATTORNEY OF ALL

A certain Jew suffered a decline in his fortune; the tide turned against him, and he found himself poor instead of rich. He came to the Ḥafetz Ḥayyim to complain of his bitter lot, that now forced his family to live in want and need. Seeking to console him, the Ḥafetz Ḥayyim told him this story:

In a certain town, two wealthy people lived. They were, however, not equally well-to-do. One owned 500,000 dollars, and the other only 200,000. One day some enemies of theirs went to the government authorities and brought charges against these two that they printed counterfeit money. Both wealthy men were arrested and imprisoned, and they languished in their cell a long time while their case was under investigation. Unable to attend to any business affairs, they found their savings dwindling at a frightening rate. Not only did their families need money to live. They also spent considerable sums in trying to establish the innocence of the two men. Needless to say, they waited impatiently for the case to come to trial.

When they had to appear in court at last, the two hired prominent defense attorneys to argue their case before the judges. As it happened, Reuven, who had originally owned 500,000 dollars, now had 200,000 left. Shimon, originally possessed of 200,000 dollars, now had but 20,000 dollars left. However, Shimon, with only 20,000 dollars left, was a good friend of a high officer in the government, and that man agreed to serve as his defense attorney.

One day during the trial, as the two sat talking together in their prison cell, Shimon said to Reuven, "With all our troubles, you are still far better off than I am. You still have 200,000 dollars left. When you go out from here a free man, you will have enough to be able to go back into business. I have only 20,000 left — far too little to let me engage in business properly. I do not know what I will be able to do."

Said Reuven, "You may think my situation is better, but you are making a mistake. You are in a better position. True, you have only a small amount of capital left. On the other hand, you have a prominent government officer representing you in court. The judges have to treat him with respect, and he will certainly get you acquitted of the charges. You are quite sure to walk out of here a free man. I hired the best lawyer I could find, but he is only an attorney. He carries no great weight with the judges. He may convince them of my innocence, and he may not. I am not too optimistic of my chances. And if the case goes against me, all the money I have left will go down the drain too. You will at least be a free man, with 20,000 dollars."

Imagine now (the Ḥafetz Ḥayyim told his visitor) that a Jew has an important dispute to settle at court, and Rambam (Maimonides) has agreed to act as his attorney. That Jew would consider himself so fortunate! It is no trifling matter to have Rambam arguing your case for you, with his brilliant mind and his superb command of the law.

Still, there is some room for doubt and worry. The Jew cannot be altogether certain of winning his case, since it may possibly turn out that he is completely in the wrong. The best attorney cannot change the facts of a case. The same holds true even if the greatest sage of the Talmud, or the Mishnah, should speak for him in court — or even a prophet. You see, we find in the Torah that even Moses our Master was not always able to win forgiveness for the people Israel.

Suppose, however, that the blessed Almighty Himself, in all His glory (as it were), consented to argue a person's case at court. Could any doubt remain then that he would receive a good verdict?

Well, Scripture tells us plainly, *He stands at the right hand of the needy, to save him from those who judge his life* (Psalms 109:31). If the Holy One Himself, in all His glory, stands at the right hand of a poor person, arguing his innocence and virtue so as to save him from those who would try him and sentence him — can you find anything better than that?

Then just think it over: What would you rather have? — a rich person's wealth, or a poor person's privilege to have the blessed Lord stand at his right to champion his cause?

77
NOT LOWER THAN THE ANGELS BUT HIGHER

As our Sages teach, the Jewish people are beloved by the Almighty, since He calls them His children (Deuteronomy 14:1). So they rank higher in Heaven's sight than the angels who dwell in the supernal realms. The angels inhabit the highest heavens, without any physical form or level of existence — beings of the purest spirituality. We human beings, on the other hand, are rooted in this lowly mundane world, encased in a physical body of flesh, sinews and bones. We are compelled to live and earn our living on this earth. Nevertheless, our service and worship is more pleasing that that of the angels, to the One whose word brought the world into being.

It can be explained by an illustration: Consider a scribe at the king's palace, and a soldier in his army, on the battlefield. Obviously both serve the king, one with his pen and one with his weapons. The scribe sits in his finely furnished palace chamber, dressed in impressive clean garments, as befits a person at the royal palace. The soldier is dressed in army clothing, dirtied in mud and filth, and often even stained with perspiration and blood.

If an outsider were to meet the two, he would certainly treat the scribe with greater respect than the soldier: The one is dressed in clothes of distinction, and the other in clothes marred by dirt and filth.

If you looked into the matter, though, you would find that the king bears a greater affection for the fighting soldier, who is always at the front, battling day after day in the war of his ruler. More than once he risks his life for the sake of his sovereign. His filthy clothing and bedraggled appearance are like a hundred witnesses, testifying that he is in the throes of battle day after day against the enemies of the king.

This is why the Jewish people are more beloved by the Almighty than the angels — because these children of His are "at the front" battling daily for the sanctification of His name (be He blessed), battling the satanic evil impulse that seeks to demolish the world. The angels, on the other hand, dwell in the lofty heights of heaven where there is no evil impulse, hence no battle and no tests of temptation to overcome.

Thus the worship and religious observance by His children in this lowly mundane world, which is the real battlefield, is far more important than the service of the angels: For we human beings sanctify His blessed name by undergoing and withstanding temptations every day, by sacrificing ourselves to keep every single mitzvah of the Torah properly. And by this we increase the power of the *shechinah*, the Divine Presence, in this world (if we may so speak). We endow the Divine retinue of the supernal realm with strength....

78

THE SINGLE, UNCHANGING WISH

A man's wants and wishes are not always the same. They change according to his needs, his physical and spiritual situation, his state of health, and so forth. A poor man beseeches the blessed Lord for an ample and respectable income. A wealthy man prays to him for greater wealth, respect, honor, and good health. A sick person prays for a full return to health. A man in a situation of peril prays to the Almighty to take him safely out of danger and bring him into a place of security.

Again, a young man and an old man will not hope and pray for the same things; nor will an ordinary person and a man of standing and high position.

Suppose, however, that we find a person who longs and hopes and prays for one and the same thing all the days of his life. He has but one request and plea to the Lord, and he never changes his mind. Then it is clear beyond the slightest doubt that this wish is the main thing in his life. This is his goal and purpose, and without it his life will have no meaning.

This is what we find with King David, the sweet singer of Israel. He prayed: *One thing have I asked of the Lord, that will I seek* (Psalms 27:4). Ever and always he had but one wish and one request — when he was a shepherd-lad in Bethlehem, king of Israel, and the singer of Israel's psalms. This was his entreaty and hope all his life, in a time of trouble and at a time of happiness, when he was abased and lowly and when he was at the height of his sovereign power. This he still sought when he was king of Israel: *that I may dwell in the house of the Lord all the days of my life, to see the graciousness of the Lord and to visit early in His temple* (*ibid.*).

This was his great enduring wish, the very root-purpose of his life, ever and always, till the end of his years.

79
THE HOME THAT WAS ENOUGH

Having heard so much of the Ḥafetz Ḥayyim as an outstanding sage of the generation, a man traveled to the town of Radun from a distant country especially to see him and speak with him. The sage's living quarters, however, took the visitor completely by surprise.

"Rabbi", he asked, "how can it be that a great man like you lives in such a poorly furnished house? You have so very little furniture, and it is in such bad condition!"

"Well, how about you?" asked the pious sage. "Do *you* have a handsome, well-furnished home here in Radun?"

"I?" answered the visitor. "I have only come for a short while. Very soon I will be leaving. Why should I need a comfortable home, for just a short stay? Any room will do."

"My dear son", said the Ḥafetz Ḥayyim, "I will tell you: All the people in this world are here just for a short stay..."

V: BETWEEN MAN AND MAN

80
THE LUCK OF LOSING ONE'S SHIRT

On the outskirts of a certain town a band of outlaws established themselves. Whenever people traveled through the surrounding forest to or from the town, these outlaws stopped them and robbed them of everything they had. So successful were they that in time a good number of idle wastrels and good-for-nothings from neighboring towns came and joined them. Soon they found that there were so many of them that it was impossible for every outlaw to know and recognize every other member of their group of robbers. There was a danger that out in the forest they might start attacking and marauding one another.

So they hit on a simple plan: They would all wear shirts of a certain color, with a little emblem. Then the bandits would always recognize their own kind.

One night a whole group of them gathered in the town saloon to pass the evening with a few drinks, and so forth. The few drinks became more and more . . . and when the time came to pay and go home, some of them found they had not brought enough money with them. The saloon-keeper had an easy answer to the problem, however: He made them leave their shirts as a pledge. When they would bring the money, said he, they would get their shirts back. Unwilling to use force against him, since the town police might then be called in against them, they did as he demanded, although they were deeply angry at him, and in their minds they vowed to take revenge.

Some time afterward the federal police discovered the secret of the shirts with the emblem — that this was what all the bandits wore so that they could identify one another. In a short while everyone wearing such a shirt found himself under arrest and in prison, and all their property and possessions were confiscated. Only a few of the outlaws went untouched: those who had been compelled to leave their shirts with the saloon-keeper. The act of the saloon-keeper, which had made them so angry, now saved them from capture by the police.

Needless to say, they were very happy. "Imagine that", they told one another. "At the time we were so angry with him for taking our shirts that we promised to take revenge. Now it turns out that he did us a tremendous favor!"

This is just how a person should feel when he knows that he has not the slightest thing in his possession acquired through any kind of theft or robbery. It is easy to feel envious of others who have amassed real wealth by sharp or shady business practices that were little short of outright robbery. Given the chance to make his own large profits in the same way, a man may well be tempted to feel entitled to go ahead, since "everybody else does the same thing". Let him know, however, that if he has a penny of stolen money in his pocket or wears a shirt with a thread in it that was gotten by robbery, in the end he will lose everything he has, and his own personal fate will be an evil one. Why? — because the Creator recognizes only too well all property gotten by robbery, and a robber's possessions are always confiscated *in toto*.

This is why the Sages of the Talmud taught that a man should be glad when the court takes away from him a garment that he took in robbery — because this simply saves his entire property from being confiscated.

81
A ROOM FOR SPIRITUAL GAIN

If the Almighty has given a man the good fortune to be able to build himself a home, he generally does not stint and confine himself to a one-room dwelling, but rather builds a house of many rooms, and sometimes even of several wings facing a courtyard; and then not all the rooms are simply to live in, but they serve a variety of purposes, according to the man's business affairs and needs.

Planning his house, it seems only natural for a man to concentrate on the physical needs: the kitchen, the living room, the dining room, the bedrooms, and so on. How very, very few ever stop and give a thought to spiritual needs, to set aside for them at least one room. Yet we know well that spiritual needs are more important and vital for a man than physical requirements: The physical self, the body, goes out of existence in time; the spirit never dies.

So we find splendid homes built, with comfortable handsome rooms for every purpose that a person may want or need — and the most important purpose of all, spiritual need, is forgotten. What room would serve that purpose? — quite simply, a room for the poor and needy, a guest room for good Jews in need of hospitality, who will otherwise go wandering about the city looking in vain for a clean warm place to rest their weary bones.

Happy and fortunate are those rare people who are also concerned with their spiritual needs, and they set apart a room for worthy guests in need of hospitality. By fulfilling the great mitzvah of being hospitable, they are privileged to receive the *shechinah*, the Divine Presence, in their home. How can anyone find greater happiness and honor than that?

82

THE PRINCESS AND THE PEASANT

A man has to be very careful not to mix or mingle with unprincipled people who commit sins without a second thought, because they are likely to turn his heart astray, veering from the ways of God, and to thrust him off the path of the Torah (Heaven forbid) until he becomes one of them. At first one may absolutely refuse to believe that this can be the result for him. How can it be, he will say, that an upstanding observant Jew who keeps the slightest mitzvah as faithfully as a serious one, can ever go off the right and decent path? It can never happen to him, he will insist. And he will go right on being friendly and carousing with worthless unprincipled louts.

This can best be explained, though, with a parable:

A king's daughter was taken captive and forced to marry an uncouth peasant lad, a lout of the coarsest and lowest type. For a long while at first, the very presence of her husband made her suffer intensely. All her life she had been accustomed to delicacy and refinement. She had lived in the lap of luxury, wearing the softest clothing of linen and silk. The palace she lived in, the food she ate, were all the finest imaginable. Try as she might, she could not grow used to the dirty, dilapidated hut, almost a barn, in which she had to live. It was torture for her to put on the rough, coarse clothing that her husband gave her. Neither could she bring herself to eat the hard black bread and coarse food that her husband always had for his meals.

She sat by the hour and wept and wailed over her bitter fate, forever groaning that death would be far better for her than a life like this.

Time works in its own way, however; and with the passage of the months, all unawares, she became accustomed to her new and unpleasant life. With each passing day she became used to the rough, simple peasant life of her husband. The hut no longer seemed so dreadfully small and miserable, the food no longer so coarse, the clothing no longer so rough and heavy to wear.

A few years went by, and it was already impossible to detect in her the delicate, refined royal princess that she had once been. To look at her you would think she had certainly been born and bred among the peasants.

A man's spirit can be compared to that princess. From a supernal mansion on high it descends to dwell in our midst, an element of Divinity in a human being. In its place of origin it lived a noble, exalted, refined existence. By Heaven's decree, however, it must spend a lifetime on earth.

Suppose now that a man makes friends with empty louts and wastrels, and begins to spend time in their company, watching them commit their transgressions and sins without end. The first time he violates a religious law and commits a wrong under their influence, it will seem to him as if a hand of his had been amputated. For the hand that committed the misdeed could hardly have been his own; and had he been in his right senses he would rather have cut it off than done such a great wrong.

The Divine spirit within him suffers agony and torment. It has the

delicacy and refinement of a princess, and cannot bear the coarse, vul-
gar food it is thus being given, or the filthy hut and execrable clothes
in which it thus has to live.

With the passage of time, however, a man becomes adjusted to his
environment and his life. The company of those irresponsible empty-
headed persons no longer troubles him. He is no longer disturbed by
the things they do. In fact, he has become one of them, to the point
where he can no longer be told apart from them. It is not possible to
recognize anymore if his spirit once had the nobility and refinement
of a royal princess, originating from a supernal source, or if it came
from a disreputable family of slaves and peasants. . . .

83
DEGREES OF INFECTION

In the world of medicine it is well known that one illness can appear
in several different forms. In one form it is a light illness, posing no
real danger. In another form it is a severe sickness, endangering the
victim's life.

Thus, for example, a man may develop a boil filled with pus, on
one of his limbs. He hurries off to see the doctor, and the doctor does
not become overly concerned. He merely lances the boil and drains
out the pus, and in a while the man is healed. In other cases a boil
may occur in a more sensitive part of the body, and there is some
danger that through the bloodstream the pus may infect the rest of
the body. Then the physician grows more concerned; but still he lances
the boil and drains out the pus; and in addition he may give his patient
medicine to help the body fight off possible infection through the bloodstream.

There can be severe advanced cases of infection, however, where a
doctor has no choice but to amputate a diseased limb so as to save a
person's life, because otherwise the infection will surely spread to the
rest of the body. And if the infection has already spread to the extent
that the body cannot overcome it, then the man's life is beyond saving.
There is no lancing or surgery that can remove the pus and the poisons
that have spread through the body.

It is the same when a man sins. If he merely commits some misdeed thoughtlessly, some part of his spiritual being, corresponding to a limb or a sinew, becomes wounded and infected, as it were. It is by no means as nothing, though. He will have to undergo suffering to be cleansed of it — like the lancing of a boil.

If, however, a man sets off on an entire program of sinning — for example, if he fills his stomach with all kinds of vile forbidden food — then the infection spreads as a poison through his spiritual self. You can well imagine what great suffering will then come upon this man, to cleanse him and purify him from the spiritual contamination of this enormous sin.

This is why a man must be extremely careful in these matters. A prudent person will stay far away from sin and spiritual illness.

84
THE LESSON OF MIRIAM

A certain man had two sons, one aged twelve, and the other ten. The first had a very sharp mind and excelled in his studies, until he became known in the entire neighborhood as a child prodigy in Talmudic learning. The second son had a normal intelligence, and was not outstanding in any way.

As his fame and reputation spread, the older boy became overbearing, and he began being haughty with his friends, treating them with a touch of scorn and vexing them. At times he went so far that, as it happens with boys, they ended with serious quarrels and fistfights.

The boy's father was not pleased with this at all. Once he simply lost his temper, whereupon he put the boy over his knee, in the presence of everyone, and gave him a good spanking — so that both he and his friends should know that he did not like his son's behavior at all.

A while later, to the father's dismay, the second son began following his older brother's example. This ordinary, undistinguished boy also began to be haughty toward his friends, lording it over them till they became vexed and irritated — in the very way that his brilliant brother behaved.

The father called his second son to him. "Listen", he said. "You saw what I did to your brother. Even though he is so very bright and has a reputation as almost a young genius in his Talmud study, I had no mercy on him. For the disgraceful way he was acting, I gave him a spanking in the presence of all his friends. Then just figure out what your punishment will be if you act like him, when you have no reputation as any kind of genius!"

In this sense Scripture says, *Remember what the Lord your God did to Miriam* (Deuteronomy 24:9). Just think it over: Miriam was the sister of Moses and Aaron, and she was herself a prophetess; and yet when she spoke evil gossip she received her punishment at once, in a way that all knew about it. How much more can we plain, ordinary people expect the same kind of result if we commit that kind of sin.

85
THE POWER OF SPEECH

Among all the creatures on earth, man alone has the power of speech, a wondrous precious gift bestowed on us by the blessed Lord, to make us the crowning achievement of His creation.

Not only is this faculty unique to man. It requires no special effort or concentration to utter a word, whereas if a person wants to do something else, he has to think and put his mind to it, to make his body obey his will. Otherwise, if he acts thoughtlessly, not only will he not succeed in doing what he wishes, but he may even come to harm.

Take for example the simple matter of driving a nail into a wall. It requires no great study or intelligence. Even a young boy can do it. Yet this plain little task requires attention and concentration. When a person holds the nail in one hand and the hammer in the other, and he hits the nail on the head with the hammer, he has to watch what he is doing and not grow absent-minded. Otherwise he can very likely hit his hand instead of the nail. And if this is true of a simple little task like that, when a trained craftsman is at work on something complicated and important, how much more certainly does he have to concentrate and keep his mind from wandering off to the slightest extent.

It is different, however, with the power of speech that the Almighty has given man. It is an amazing faculty of the human being, requiring no special attention or concentration when a man wants to use it. There is no need to beware of letting our attention wander — and this despite the fact that making the sounds of speech is no simple matter but is quite complicated, requiring the exact coordination of lips, tongue, palate, vocal cords, and so on.

Why was speech made so automatic a faculty? — because when a person utters a word, he has to bear in mind what it means; and for this he has to focus his thought — so that there is no room left in his mind to concentrate at the same time on the proper way to produce the right sounds for the word. It is well known that the mind cannot think of two things at the same time. Therefore, since we cannot keep our attention simultaneously on both the meaning of a word and the production of its sound, the Almighty endowed us with this wondrous gift, that the sounds of the letters form by themselves for us, needing no special focus of mind. So in one minute a person has the ability to utter some 200 words, provided he pays attention to their meaning.

Had the Almighty not given us this great faculty, we would be able to learn in the course of a day no more than one chapter of Torah; and at times one chapter might take several days.

Well, therefore a man is commanded to guard and watch this precious gift in every possible way, so that he will not use it for any sinful purpose, such as evil gossip, slander, lies, scornful and insulting "humor", and similar sins of the tongue. For if a man commits such transgressions, he misuses tragically the gift with which the Almighty has endowed him so that he can study the Torah and keep the commandments that apply to the power of speech.

Thus, in the first paragraph of Sh'ma yisrael we read, and you shall talk of them (Deuteronomy 6:7); whereupon the Sages comment, "of them, and not of idle matters". In idle or sinful chatter, a person uses for evil the good faculty that the Almighty has given him.

86
YOU GET AS YOU GIVE

The leading members of the Jewish community of Bialystok once as-

sembled to consider ways and means of strengthening and supporting
the Council of Yeshivoth, which was responsible for maintaining the
Torah schools and academies. The Ḥafetz Ḥayyim, who had founded
the Council, attended the meeting. Immediately afterward, by invitation,
all the wealthy and distinguished members of the community came
together at the Ḥafetz Ḥayyim's hotel, where he stayed while in Bialystok; and every single one of them obligated himself to donate a
certain amount of money, according to his means, for the Council of
Yeshivoth.

One rich man, however, absolutely refused to give anything. "Look
at these", he said. "Here you have a whole collection of receipts for
the donations I have given over the years to various yeshivoth in this
city. Examine them and add up the amounts, and then tell me if you
think I have not done my duty to keep the mitzvah of supporting
Torah study." He set down a whole packet of receipts before the rabbis and distinguished Jews, and then he sat back, immovable as stone.

Had the Ḥafetz Ḥayyim himself been there, perhaps the man would
not have been so brazen. The pious sage, however, was in his hotel
room resting, and the others could do nothing with him. A few men
slipped quietly out of the conference room and went to see the Ḥafetz
Ḥayyim. He came down at once and entered the conference room.
Slowly he went to the head of the table to speak, and the room fell
silent. Turning to the stubborn man of wealth, the pious sage said, "I
am told that you argue that you have already fulfilled your obligation
to support the study of Torah. Well, now, you ought to know that
there are various ways in which a man can fulfill his obligation.

"For example, a person has to eat. It is possible to make do with
coarse bread, potatoes, and a bowl of soup — day after day. There
are many in our land who never taste anything else during their lives.
Tens of thousands have meat only once or twice a week; many others,
even less often. And they too fulfill their obligation to keep themselves
fed.

"The same holds true with living quarters: A family of ten can
manage to live in an apartment of one room. Many live out their entire
lives under such conditions, and they are perfectly healthy.

"Then there is the obligation to wear clothing: Who says that a man has to have suits and shirts of fine, expensive cloth, and a fur-lined coat? Farmers and peasants wear garments of rough homespun cloth, and rope-sandals on their feet. And so they make do.

"However, you, my dear sir, would not wish to get by and fulfill your obligation like that. You want nothing less than loaves out of fine white flour every day, with chicken soup and roast meat. You want a splendid spacious home of six or seven rooms, lit by electric lights, warmed by central heating. You dress in fine expensive clothes and spend a tidy sum for a pair of shoes.

"Well, truth to tell, you are doing nothing wrong by living on this standard. A man ought to live in the style to which the Almighty's providence entitles him, not just to 'fulfill his obligation' and get by on a minimum. If the good Lord has blessed someone's business enterprise and he earns a handsome, comfortable income, he has the right to enjoy God's bounty. Everything He created in His world is for the enjoyment of His human beings. However, my dear sir: in that case, if a Jew lives and supports his family on a standard that does not merely fulfill his obligation, then his gifts to charity and his donations to support Torah study also have to be more than merely enough to fulfill his obligation.

"For what, my good man, do you think will be the end of the matter? I will tell you", said the Ḥafetz Ḥayyim. "After your span of years you will leave this world and pass on to the world of truth, and you will stand before Heaven's court of justice. Then they will ask you: 'Tell us, sir: Did you give money for charitable causes? Did you support the scholars and students devoted to the study of the Torah?' Of course, you will do there what you did here. You will take out at once your pile of receipts for all your donations, and you will say, 'Gentlemen, honored members of the court, here you have my receipts. I have fulfilled my obligation.'

"Do you know what they will do? They will tell you, 'Splendid. Indeed you fulfilled your obligation. You did your duty.' And they will take you at once right into paradise, the Garden of Eden, where you will see a large group of people seated around a table of gold, enjoying the radiance and luster of the *shechinah*, the Divine Presence. You will take a good look, and you will see that those people are mighty, profound Torah scholars, together with men who gave *generously* to support Torah study, far more than just enough to fulfill their obligation and do their duty. You will want to join them, to take your place at that enchanting table. Instead, however, you will find yourself led off into a corner, where you will remain standing; and no one will pay the slightest attention to you.

"Of course, you will be amazed and perplexed, and immediately you will complain to the management: 'I also gave my charity. I donated handsomely to yeshivoth, to support the study of Torah!' And you will hold out and wave your fine collection of receipts.

"Do you know what they will answer you? 'Take it easy, dear sir. What are you shouting about? You gave enough to fulfill your obligation? You are receiving enough of a share here, in the Garden of Eden, to fulfill *our* obligation.' And that will be that."

87
IF NOT ALL, THEN NOTHING?

People have often become dismayed at the prospect of giving and giving to the poor. They have simply given up trying to give enough to help their penniless and needy brethren, because they see so many of them. There seem to be more and more demands for charity every day, until it becomes virtually impossible to help everyone and give to every deserving cause. Since they cannot give everyone and everywhere, to relieve all the needy and the distressed, they simply give up and decide to give no charity at all. As it were, they put up a sign reading, *The charity department is closed.*

What are those people like? Let us answer with a parable:

A man once watched a bridge over a river swaying dangerously in the wind, and to his horror it collapsed, flinging some twenty persons into the swiftly coursing river. There they thrashed about, in danger of drowning. Two people at the shore swiftly dived into the river and swam out to save some of them.

"Don't be foolish!" the man who was watching called out to them.

"What's the use of jumping into the water? Can you possibly save them all? There are only two of you, and twenty of them. It is better to stay on shore and not get involved. Keep out of it altogether!"

Was he right? Did his advice make any sense? Is it not worthwhile to go to every trouble and make every effort to save two people out of twenty, or even one? Granted that there is no hope of saving all the twenty. Does that justify a person in standing aside and abandoning to their death the few whom he could save?

This is something a man must always bear well in mind. He has to do all he can to help and rescue, to the full extent of his ability.

88
THE PARTNERSHIP

Two men, Reuven and Shimon, were partners in a business; and their arrangement was that during the year each would draw out of the business a fixed amount of money every week — enough to support their families. At the end of the year they would calculate the profit that the business earned, and this they would divide equally.

Time went by, and the business took a serious turn for the worse. The situation became so bad that they faced virtual bankruptcy. When the two partners saw this, Reuven told Shimon, "Look: we have to reduce our expenses at home and live on very little, until we can get the business doing well again." Shimon agreed.

In the weeks that followed, Reuven economized at home in every possible way, until his weekly expenses were a third of what they had been. With Shimon, however, it was a different story: With his mouth he had agreed to economize, but privately he thought it was nonsense: Why economize? The business would surely recover.... He continued to live as lavishly as before, and even increased his weekly expenditures a bit; and whatever money he needed, he simply drew out of the business funds without letting Reuven know.

The business did not get better, however, but became worse, earning them less money than ever before. In desperation the partners sat down to go over the books carefully, to see if there was any way out of their predicament. The figures in the account books told their own story, and it did not take Reuven long to realize what Shimon had been doing: that not only had he not learned to economize and reduce the amount of money he drew from the business every week, but he had been taking more and more each week for his living expenses. Reuven had taught his family to live almost in complete poverty, with just enough for their barest needs; and Shimon's family had been living in luxury.

"Robber! Thief!" shouted Reuven. "All along you have been fooling me! Here my family and I have been living almost in want, because I economized; and you and your family have been living just fine! You never cared one bit for the business. When it was doing so badly, you just went and helped bury it. Do you know what is left for me to do? I have to start making the rounds through the streets, knocking on doors, to ask for charity!"

It is this very argument and contention that the quality or duty of charity can present against a person. For evidently this too is a matter of partnership: The Almighty gives a man all he needs for both "partners": for his own sustenance and needs, and for gifts to charity. So a man has an obligation to give a share of his income to charity, as the Sages ruled.

Now, if he sees that hard times have come and his earnings grow smaller, he has to practice economy for both "partners": His family and he must learn to live on less, and he must reduce his donations to charity, until the Almighty improves his situation and makes him affluent again. For after all, it is a partnership.

Too many people, however, behave as Shimon did. For himself he did not economize at all; in fact, he learned to spend more, so that his family and he could live better. And he left all the stinting and economizing for his partner to do, even if it meant doing without the bare necessities. So also, far too many people stop giving anything to the poor and stop supporting the students and the study of Torah, giving only a few meager pennies to charity now and then.

Do you think charity will remain a "silent" partner and say nothing? Do you think it will keep silent and not bring any bitter complaint before Heaven against its mistreatment?

89

THE TRAITOROUS QUARTERMASTER

In a certain country the king raised one of his army officers to the rank of quartermaster of his fighting forces. Unfortunately, the promotion went to the man's head. He began putting on airs and acting in a grand, lordly manner, in keeping (as he thought) with his new position and his new ample salary.

That was not all, however. His ideas of how a quartermaster should live became so grandiose that soon his new ample salary was not enough for him, and he felt forced to use government funds that were entrusted to him for the expenses of the army. The result was that in a while the soldiers began to be underfed, till they felt the pinch of hunger; and when there were special tasks to be done, such as digging ditches or building roads, instead of hiring work crews, as he should have done, the high and mighty quartermaster set the soldiers to this back-breaking work, so as to save money — the money that he always needed to funnel into his own pocket, for his living expenses.

One fine day the king decided to visit one of the army divisions, to see for himself how the soldiers were faring: if they were satisfied with army life, and if their general was satisfied with them. As he went about on his inspection, he called several soldiers over to him. "Tell me", he said. "How do you find life in the army? Are you reasonably satisfied? Do you get enough to eat?"

The men hesitated to tell the king the truth. The quartermaster might learn of what they said, and he could penalize them severely. Two soldiers were courageous, however, and they stepped forward to reply:

"Your majesty, we literally suffer hunger. We do not get half the food we need to keep our strength up. And on top of that, we are worked hard at tasks that soldiers should not be expected to do. The result is that we are simply losing our strength and our health."

The king stroked his beard in surprise. Could it be? Was the man telling the truth? There was a simple way to find out. He sent for a staff of physicians and ordered them to examine the soldiers. Soon enough he had their report: The two soldiers had told the truth: The men were weak because they were undernourished, and many were on the verge of serious illness.

It did not take the king long to discover that no one but the quartermaster was responsible for this. In a furious rage the king sent for him, and in the presence of the full army he stripped him of his rank, dismissed him from the armed forces, and rebuked and disgraced him roundly.

Then he turned to the troops massed in formation before him. "Is there anyone here who is ready to take on this man's job? Is any of you ready to serve as our army quartermaster?" One soldier stepped out of line and marched up, to offer his services; and the king gave him the position.

To everyone's surprise, the man did his work quite well. Conscientious and devoted, unafraid of hard work, he rode about to the army bases and inspected the food supplies and the kitchen equipment, taking careful note of what was needed. A month or two went by, and the effect of his work began to be seen, in the meals that the soldiers received, and in the non-soldierly kinds of work that they no longer had to do.

When the king learned the results of the new man's work since he began serving as quartermaster, he called the former quartermaster to him and became angry at him all over again: "You empty lout! You good-for-nothing! You took a large salary, and it was not enough for you. You stole government funds for yourself and starved the soldiers. Now a plain soldier comes along, earning a plain soldier's salary, and in a few weeks he clears up and corrects your mismanagement of many long months. What did you imagine? — that all the funds you received out of the government treasury were for your own benefit and pleasure? Do you mean to tell me that you never realized that the funds were to supply the army with food? You are a traitor to your country and your king. As of now you are under arrest. You will be brought to trial and given the punishment you deserve."

Every Jew who receives any degree of wealth by the Almighty's blessing, is a kind of quartermaster. He has to know that he is only a steward or caretaker over the money that he has amassed, and it is to be used for charity: to treat with kindness the Almighty's army of human beings, created in His image. Should a person act like the quartermaster above, imagining himself entitled to use the money for his personal benefit and pleasure, and giving none of it to others even if they are dying of hunger — he can be assured that he will come to a bitter end. Sooner or later the money will be taken from him and given to someone else, who will know how to use it wisely, properly and humanely.

90
ON COMPETITION AND QUARRELING

As a family once sat down at the table to have a meal, a quarrel broke out between two children over their food. One insisted that the other received a larger portion than he did; and as he wept and complained, without any great preparations he simply stood up, reached out, and seized his brother's portion.

At that the second brother turned to his father: "Did you see that, father? The portion that I was given, he simply took and snatched away. I could have a fight with him and take it back by force if I wanted to, because I am stronger. I won't do that, though, because I know you don't want us to quarrel and fight and come to fist-blows. Then let me ask you to please let me have a different portion — and that will be that."

The father praised his son's conduct; and he told him, "Since you refrained from fighting with your brother, you deserve a larger portion than the one he took from you; and that is what you are going to get."

Had the boy not been tolerant and self-controlled; had he continued the quarrel till it developed into a fist-fight and wrestling-match — the father would have vented his anger on both of them, even though the second brother was originally not at fault — because a father is never pleased at quarrels and conflicts among his children.

Well, it is the same in regard to provision and sustenance. We read in *Tanna d'vey Eliyahu* (chapter 28): The Holy Blessed One said to the Jewish people, "My beloved children, have I left you lacking in what I ask of you? For after all, what do I ask of you? — only that you should love one another . . . and no sin or robbery should be found among you. . . ."

When a man is grasping and rapacious, whatever he has is never enough for him. He casts his eyes on what another person has, till he goes and virtually steals the food out of another's mouth. He competes with the other person viciously, giving the other one's merchandise a bad name, so as to draw the customers to him — to increase his profits and his income at the other one's expense.

Suppose now that the other person, the victim of his cut-throat competition, avoids any kind of argument, quarrel or contention with him. He does not take him to court; he does not descend to spreading evil gossip or slander about the man, but simply stands and pours out his entreaty before the blessed Lord: "O Sovereign of the world, this portion of sustenance that You did give me — this way of earning my living — my fellow-man came with tactics of chicanery and robbery, and took it away from me! I know very well that I am in the right and he is in the wrong. Yet I know also that it is not Your wish to have us quarrel and come to a serious conflict. Therefore I pray You: Give me another way of sustenance, another way of earning my living, so that my family and I shall not perish from hunger."

Past any doubt the blessed Lord will give him his measure of provision and sustenance — even more than he received before.

Suppose, however, that the man becomes involved in quarrels and conflicts with his vicious, predatory competitor. Suppose he takes him to court, and through the open strife and ugly arguments, the name of God is desecrated. Then we must expect Him to become enraged (so to speak) at both — even at the victim, who in effect has been robbed by the cut-throat competition, although he is apparently free of any blame. And it is easy to surmise that if He (as it were) grows angry at them, neither of them will ever find any really good fortune in the world.

91
NOT TO LOSE THE LIFELINE

Since time immemorial, banks, large and small, have been part of human society and its urban communities. As a rule, small banks always drew their income by a link with larger banks, borrowing funds from them, which they would then relend to small businessmen, partnerships, and so forth.

Should a large bank ever fail and go bankrupt, it would drag down many small banks with it; and these banks would draw down the many business establishments that needed and used their loans to continue operating.

Now, who is the biggest banker in the world, operating the largest bank of all? — the Almighty; for we read, *Mine is the silver, and Mine the gold, says the Lord* (Haggai 2:8). This means that He (so to speak) is the ultimate unique source for all the silver and gold to be found anywhere, in the possession of anyone in the entire world. It is He who bestows poverty and wealth. He provides the sustenance for all living beings, from the horned buffalo to the larvae of vermin. He opens His hand and satisfies every living creature. Should the Almighty wish (Heaven forbid) to shut His hand, so to speak, and remove His watchful care from a man for a split second, in an instant that man can change from the richest person in the world to a penniless beggar making the rounds and knocking on doors. All depends on His will.

Well, the Sages taught (Talmud, Avodah Zarah 18): Said R. Katina: Whoever speaks in derisive jest and mockery, his sustenance is reduced. He will eventually find himself earning less; as Scripture says, *He withdraws His hand from scorners* (Hosea 7:5); and Rashi explains that this means the same metaphoric hand with which He sustains and satisfies every living being.

So anyone who occupies himself with mockery and scorn, or who takes his place among scoffers and people of derision, cuts himself off with his own hands from the unique ultimate source of his income and livelihood; and he is likely to lose everything he has — because the Almighty withdraws His hand from him.

It is therefore up to a man to be very careful not to come to grief
with this severe and serious sin.

92
A POINT OF VIEW

Once, as a result of circumstances, Reuven decided that Shimon had
done him a great injustice deliberately, and he could not find it in his
heart to forgive the man.

One day Reuven was walking in the street, when he met Levi, one
of his good friends, whom he knew to be a decent, honest man. Since
the matter weighed on his heart, Reuven told Levi of the series of
events that made him decide that Shimon had deliberately done him
a serious wrong. "I cannot forgive him for it", Reuven added, "because when I told him of it he would not admit that justice is on my
side — and it clearly is so."

"Do you know Shimon at all?" asked Levi. "Do you know what
sort of man he is, that you can be so sure that he could act so badly
toward you? I will tell you: A few days ago, by chance I saw him
sitting with the great Talmud scholar, Rabbi So-and-so, who is known
as a man of deep piety; and the rabbi treated him with considerable
respect."

"Oh yes?" asked Reuven, and he remained thoughtful. He knew
Levi too well as a man of integrity, to doubt his word to the slightest
extent. "Do you know?" he said at last. "Now a shade of doubt has
entered my mind: Maybe I was not really right in my quarrel with
Shimon. Till now I was absolutely sure of it. I could see no justification
for the way he acted toward me. Since you told me this about him,
however, I have begun to wonder: Am I mistaken in some way?"

A few days later the two friends met again. "Do you know?" said
Levi. "Yesterday I saw Shimon again; he was sitting with those two
famous authorities in religious law, Rabbi So-and-so and Rabbi So-
and-so; and both of them received him cordially and accorded him
great respect."

At that Reuven was filled with contrition and remorse. "Woe is
me!" he cried. "What a great sin I have committed against Shimon.

Surely a man like that must have been right in the way he treated me in our dispute. I must have been wrong, and I simply didn't see it. How could I have misjudged him, if he is such a fine man? How could I have made such a bad mistake?"

It happens that sometimes two persons turn against each other, remaining mutually hostile and antagonistic; and they bear each other a bitter grudge for years. A man may ask a neighbor to lend him something, and the neighbor will refuse, whereupon he becomes an implacable enemy of his neighbor, ready to tear him apart.

If only everyone were ready to regard his neighbor as a person on a higher level than himself, he would surely be able to find some defense or explanation for his neighbor's behavior, and justify him — and thus he could accept him with favor and live in peace.

93
THE ART OF SALESMANSHIP

The Torah commands us to rebuke and reprove a fellow-Jew if we see him committing a wrong or sinful deed. Sometimes, as we try our best to dissuade him from going ahead and doing the bad deed, we may not find it an easy task. We may find that he simply will not listen. Let us not give up hope then, or give way to grief or despair. We certainly cannot expect it to be easy work at all.

Consider a storekeeper who is interested in selling as much of his merchandise as he can. Suppose a difficult customer comes in. Would it occur to the storekeeper to grow angry with the man because he is hard to please and wants to pick and choose, or he bargains a long time over the price? Should it occur to him to refuse to sell anything to the man because he is being difficult? Did you ever in your life see a storekeeper hang up a sign like this in his shop-window: "Here we sell only to good, pleasant, easy customers. No sales to tough customers"?

Certainly there are no merchants or storekeepers like that. A man who wants to sell his goods and wares has to be tolerant and easygoing by nature. He has to use tact and persuasion, speaking gently and patiently till he prevails on his customer to buy. Otherwise he will not earn his living.

Well, when a man wishes to induce someone to do a mitzvah, a religious good deed, he is like a storekeeper trying to sell his merchandise. For he too stands to earn profit, since great reward awaits those who bring others to observe a mitzvah. So if there are those who listen and accede to him at once, like customers who enter a store and buy a piece of merchandise readily, without bargaining, well and good. If some, however, are not receptive and will not yield — like burdensome, recalcitrant customers who do not find the merchandise to their liking and are inclined to bargain heavily before they agree on the price — a person who would induce and sway them to observe the Torah must know and understand that it is worth investing effort to "sell" to them also. There is spiritual "profit" to be made. And ultimately these "customers" too will "buy" something. . . .

94
THE NEED TO KEEP SELLING

Scripture says literally, *You shall reprove, reprove your neighbor* (Leviticus 19:17). As the verb is doubled, the Talmud (Bava M'tzi'a 31) interprets it to mean: even a hundred times.

Certainly it cannot be pleasant for a person to rebuke a man and speak to him of ethics and morals when he sees that all his efforts are in vain and his words are simply falling on deaf ears. We have to learn a valuable lesson, however, from the kind of woman who stands in the marketplace selling apples. All day long she stands on her feet by her basket of apples, calling out, "Apples for sale! Buy my apples, cheap!"

Once a man passed by a woman like that, and out of curiosity he stood off in a corner and watched. She never stopped calling and crying her wares, although in all the time he watched her, he saw not one person stop and buy anything from her. She sold not one piece of fruit, yet she kept exclaiming, "Apples, cheap!"

At last the man went over to her: "Tell me, my dear woman. I have been watching you for a good long while now, and listening to you shout the whole place down, telling the world that you have apples for sale. Yet in all this time no one came and bought even a penny's worth!"

The woman laughed. "Bless you", she said. "What do you think I make my living from, if not from these apples? Every evening I go home and count the money I have taken in during the day. A little of it is profit — enough for a loaf of bread and a bowl of soup. Out of a hundred people who pass by my basket of fruit, one is bound to come over and buy some. At times even one out of ten will come and buy my apples. It all depends on my luck, you might say. But heavens! If I ever stopped shouting my wares, who would ever know that I was there with my basket of apples, and how would I earn my living?"

It is somewhat the same in giving reproof. When a man rebukes some-one to lead him onto the right path, he is doing an important mitzvah, and is assured of great reward for it. It is very possible that ninety-nine people out of a hundred will pay no attention either to him or to his reproving talk. They will not heed him, and in fact may even scorn and mock him. Yet should he succeed in returning even one person alone to the good path, his reward will be plentiful indeed.

If, however, a man is too bashful or lazy to call aloud about his "merchandise", it is quite certain that no one will know about him. Then from what will he earn his spiritual "living"?

VI: REWARD AND PUNISHMENT

95

THE MOUTHFUL OF FLESH

There was a king who had one true, close friend, to whom he revealed his innermost thoughts. From this friend he kept nothing back, neither government secrets nor personal matters. He was very devoted to the friend, and would not move hand or foot in running the country without consulting him.

The time came, however, when the king discovered to his consternation that this "dear friend" of his was a vile traitor: For a high price he sold important state secrets to another king, who was hostile to this royal sovereign. The proof of his treachery was undeniable, leaving not the shadow of a doubt. More than anger at finding his friend so false to him, the king felt a pain and an ache. Nevertheless, he was determined to pass a severe sentence against the traitor, that would serve as a lesson to anyone who might contemplate rebellion or espionage. He would make this man's name a reviled byword for all time.

What did he do? He ordered a large structure, with all its walls of transparent glass, erected in the central square of the capital city. It was to be a prison cell, where the traitor was to be kept locked in until he died of hunger and thirst. Heralds and messengers brought the king's proclamation to all the people to come and see the punishment of the scoundrel.

The king's orders were carried out to the letter. The glass prison cell was constructed, and there the condemned man was brought. And every day a huge crowd assembled to watch his slow but certain end.

The first day, the prisoner was in good spirits. Before being taken to his new place of detention he had been given a sumptuous meal. So he was able to sit on a soft comfortable chair, reading a book, as the huge crowd watched him in curiosity. The second day, however, signs of worry and sorrow began to appear on his face. Hunger was beginning to trouble him. Ever so often the people outside saw him get up and pace the floor of his glass cell restlessly.

The third day, the crowd saw a crestfallen man haunted by fear. The prisoner's hands shook as he watched, with burning eyes, the sight of people in the group eating sandwiches and fruit, and so forth. The fourth day, he could hardly stand upright on his feet. He walked with difficulty, with faltering footsteps, leaning on the wall to keep from falling. On the fifth and sixth days he could not get up at all. The gathered people saw him lying on the floor, writhing in the throes of intense hunger.

It was on the seventh day that a dreadful thing occurred: Before the horrified eyes of the crowd of spectators, the prisoner tore his clothes from him, stuck his teeth into his arm, tore out a mouthful of his own flesh, and began chewing voraciously.

As it happened, that day a man arrived in the capital city from an outlying village at the country's border. The king's proclamation about the traitor had reached his village a bit late, and he had set off at once for the capital to see the sight. In great curiosity he pushed his way through the crowd, till he had a full view of the prisoner.

He looked, and could not believe his eyes. According to the proclamation, the man should have received no food for the past week. Yet there he sat chewing away. Perplexed, the country visitor asked a man nearby, "Tell me, good friend: Is that the man who was sentenced to be starved to death because he was the king's closest friend and he betrayed him?"

"Oh yes", said the other. "That certainly is the man."

"Then what in the world is he eating? It seems to be a piece of meat!"

"Don't be a fool", said the other man, laughing. "Can't you see that the man is eating his own flesh, from his own body?"

What is the moral of the story? We often see really strange and puzzling things in the ways of the world. There are wicked people who violate every law in the Torah, who have never observed the slightest mitzvah; and they seem to enjoy a good life in every respect. They live in pleasure and ease, eating meat, drinking wine, basking in every kind of luxury. On the other hand, utterly good and pious people live out their days in difficulty and poverty, barely able to manage.

Well, these matters appear puzzling and hard to understand only when a person sees nothing but the surface, what appears superficially to the eye. If someone takes the trouble to probe and see behind the surface, he will find that metaphorically speaking, the wicked eat nothing more than their own flesh.

96

THE WATCHFUL OWNER OF THE ORCHARD

A man once owned a beautiful orchard on a handsome stretch of ground, that yielded the finest fruit. Within the orchard he built himself a sturdy summer-house, so that he could rest there, enjoying the clear fresh air and the captivating scenery.

On a quiet afternoon he sat in the summer-house, looking out the window and feasting his eyes on the beautiful trees laden with ripe fruit. Suddenly he noticed a man forcing his way into the orchard through a break in the fence. The man went over to a particularly fine apple tree, set a basket on the ground, and began picking apples from the tree and putting them in the basket.

The owner of the orchard did nothing. He continued sitting at his window and watching in silence, curious to see what would happen. After a short while he heard the thief sigh: "Why should I tire myself out picking these apples one by one? Wouldn't it be easier just to break off branches with all the apples on them?"

No sooner said than done. The man began breaking off branches laden with apples and making a pile of them. This made the owner grow furious as he watched through the window. Yet he still kept his peace and made not a sound. A few moments later, however, he heard the impudent thief sighing again: "What a fool I am. Why bother breaking off branches? I have this sturdy basket on wheels. Let me just chop the whole tree down and take it with me, on the basket."

Again, no sooner said than done — or at least he tried. He went to his basket to take out an axe. Now, however, the owner was absolutely unable to keep still. He ran to the thief, seized him by the collar of his shirt, and began shouting at him, "You wicked scoundrel! You vile thief! When I saw you sneaking into the orchard and gathering apples, I thought you might be a poor person with a wife and children, and you wanted a little fruit for your family to eat. Well and good, I thought: Go ahead and take some. Then I saw you start breaking off branches. I became angry, but decided to restrain myself. Perhaps, I thought, you would not take too many branches. Now you want to chop down the tree? And then what? You will come back every day and chop down another tree, till I will have no orchard left? And do you think I will just sit by my window and watch? For an outrage like this I cannot forgive you. You are going with me to the police, and you will pay your penalty in full!"

There are wicked people enough in the world, who refuse to follow the good ways of the Almighty. At first they decide to violate the "fences", the laws and rules set by the Sages of the Talmud — the extra, added restrictions. They will not damage the main plants of the vineyard or trees of the orchard: the actual laws of the Torah itself.

Once they see, however, that when they violate the "fences" of our great Sages, no one rises up to protest or to try to stop them, they become bold and arrogant, and they reach out to begin "breaking off branches": They start to violate explicit commands and prohibitions of the Torah. They do not put on t'fillin. They go and eat non-kosher food openly; and so on.

Having become accustomed to such deeds of sin, their heart grows proud and overweening in boastful self-confidence. Then they go on to main laws and principles of the Torah. They violate the most sacred and treasured tenets and practices of our faith.

Can anyone believe for a moment that the "owner of the orchard", the Almighty who gave the Torah, will simply watch this and be still and do nothing? He will most certainly settle accounts with the wicked, with the full severity of the law. He will make them pay for the disgrace that the Torah suffers at their hands.

97

THE WELL-TREATED AND THE BADLY-TREATED

A mighty king once decided to treat with great favor the family of a
certain nobleman who died. The nobleman had been a close friend in
his youth, and had served him faithfully as an officer and member of
the royal court. The king therefore remained most friendly to the
family, granting it a large landed estate as a permanent possession,
and appointing the young men in the family to positions of high office,
prestige and power. In fact, if there was anything that a member of
the family wanted, he had only to ask, and the king granted him his
wish.

It is small wonder then that all the members of the family were
fiercely loyal to the king, and they served him faithfully, caring only
for his good and the welfare of his country. As long as they lived, the
king knew he could depend on their devotion.

The first generation died off, however. Those whom the king benefited
directly and raised to high rank, passed away. Their sons took their
place; but those sons felt altogether differently about the king. With
prestige and power in their hands, they hatched a secret plot to foment
a rebellion against him and remove him from the throne. As it turned
out, however, their plot was discovered.

So strong was the king's affection for the family that he decided to
be lenient and overlook the situation. He merely sent high-ranking
distinguished officers to the young would-be rebels in the family, to
rebuke them and talk persuasively until they realized what a great
wrong they had done: Through all the years, the king had treated the
family with nothing but kindness and good; and now they rose up in
place of their parents, and decided to repay his kindness with hostility
and evil.

The officers went and spoke long and earnestly with the young men;
but it was all in vain. The young men were convinced that the king
was bad for the country, and had to be removed from the throne for
the good of the land. . . . It was clear that as long as the young men
remained at liberty, they would work to foment a revolution. In fact,
they insisted on surrounding themselves with a host of followers, and

began training them into a fighting force. The king was left with no choice but to send his army to squash the whole thing permanently. The would-be revolution was stamped out; the plotters and leaders were put under arrest, and they were sentenced to death. The time of execution, however, was set for some months ahead.

A few weeks later, the king sent one of his court attendants to see how the prisoners were faring in their dungeon, in the short time that was left them to live. The man went, and he found that the prisoners were being treated miserably: housed in small, dark miserable cells, fed very poorly, and so forth.

The court attendant came back and reported it all; and he added, "Your majesty, if you would permit me, may I say that I think it is a great injustice. Surely it is enough that these revolutionaries have been sentenced to death. Should they also be subject to suffering and torment until the day of their death? They have so little time left to live. I believe it would be only just to let them live out these days in comfort and ease, with good food to sustain them."

"Yes", said the king, "you are quite right. Yet I will not be equally kind with all of them. I believe you know how dearly I loved that family, how great were the favors that I bestowed on them. Even now my heart grieves at their fate. I suffer at the thought of the bitter end that awaits them so very soon. Yet this I also know: Although they were all partners in the plot and all were equally determined to hatch a revolution, not all of them were hostile toward me. A few of them were vile scoundrels, who meant me harm personally. They must die. Many among them, however, had no ill will toward me. They remained loyal to me personally, in spite of everything; and when they turned rebels, they were not themselves to blame. The others, the few vicious scurrilous characters, turned their heads and convinced them, with a great deal of claptrap, that I have to be removed for the good of the country. Now, I am quite certain, they are sorry for what they have done, and would like to make amends.

"Well then", continued the king, "this is what I will do: I will have a new, thorough investigation made by some of my trusted men, to find out for certain just which ones among them were the real plotters and fomenters of trouble who were behind the whole thing from the start; and who were merely pulled along in their wake and persuaded to act with more emotion than reason. The real plotters and trouble-makers will go to their death, of course. The others, who are still loyal to me despite everything, will live. I shall grant them a pardon and set them free. And I shall even give them back their positions in my government, so that they can serve me as before. The time they have spent in the prison is punishment enough for the wrong they have done. And I know they will bear me more affection and loyalty than before, because they will remember that over and above the favors of the past that I granted them, there is this greatest kindness of all: I freed them from their death sentence.

"This, then", said the king, "is what we shall do: Whoever is found by the investigation to have been one of the true rebels — a scoundrel who must die — I will order him treated royally in the prison until the day of his execution. He will have the finest food and drink, what-ever his heart desires. He will be given a soft comfortable bed for sleeping. Why not? The poor devil will soon be dead anyway. That is punishment enough. Let him really enjoy his last few days of life. The others, however, who are going to be set free, will continue to suffer in the prison. Let them go on eating a miserable inadequate diet and sleeping on a board in a dingy little cell. In that way they will pay for the lesser crime that they committed."

The king's wishes were carried out without delay. In a few days the investigation was completed. The prisoners were told nothing, but a few of them were singled out for "royal treatment": They had lavish meals and comfortable beds for the night. The others were treated as wretchedly as before.

The result was that the first group, under "royal treatment", became full of scorn and derision toward the other prisoners: "Take a good look at yourselves", they laughed. "Here you have spent days and nights weeping your hearts out in bitter regret and remorse because you joined us in plotting the rebellion. You have been so sorry that you ever joined us and turned against your precious king, whom you love so much. We never regretted turning against him. We are not sorry but proud of what we did. And now do you see? The king honors us and treats us splendidly, while he pays not the slightest attention to you. He doesn't care if you are almost starving here!"

One among the other prisoners understood, however, what the king intended. He waited till the others, who were receiving the special treatment, finished laughing. Then he said, "Gentlemen, he laughs best who laughs last. When you are so happy and cheerful now, do you think *we* are the fools? How much real enjoyment can you have from your fancy meals and comfortable beds when you know that your days are numbered? If the king really wanted to be kind to you, he would set you free. You are still in prison, as much as before — which means that he plans to have his revenge; and in the midst of all your fine living and good enjoyment you are going to meet your end.

"As for us", he continued, "we agree that the king isn't coddling us and giving us fancy treatment. To my mind that means one thing: He intends to let us go free. I think he knows how sorry we are that we ever listened to you ringleaders and turned against him. He knows how broken in spirit we are over it, how we have even wept and grieved over it — because we remember all the good he did for our family since ever so long ago. So he keeps us here in this dungeon under the same miserable conditions as before, to make us pay *in this way* for our crime. I for one am sure, however, that the time is coming very soon when we will be leaving this prison as free men. And then, I believe and hope, we will be able to serve our dear king as faithfully and loyally as before."

The moral of the story is evident enough. The blessed Lord chose our forefathers to be His treasured people. He treated them with abounding kindness: He rescued them from slavery into freedom, He took them out of the Egyptian house of bondage, and brought them to Him. He gave them the holy Torah, which remains the repository of our wisdom and understanding in the eyes of all the nations. He gave them a spacious good and cherished land for an inheritance, driving out before them the seven heathen nations that occupied it beforehand.

Our forefathers used to give praise and thanks to His great name for all the good He had done for them. They kept His commandments and remained loyal to His covenant, His solemn agreement with them. With the passage of time, however, the children and later generations who arose in their place began to behave in evil ways in His sight. Having been treated so well that they prospered in great comfort, they kicked out and rebelled. They abandoned His Torah and refused to follow His ways.

Many went astray from the proper path that He showed them. A great part of them, however, only wandered off by mistake, having been misguided and misled by people intent on going and leading others astray. So the blessed Lord sent His messengers, His holy prophets, to turn them back to the good way. The prophets came to remind the descendants of Abraham, Isaac and Jacob of the immutable, unchanging Lord who had made them His people and had formed a covenant with them. They shut their ears, however, and would not listen.

Then the Almighty sent His harsh, punitive messengers: the heathen kings and their armies. As we read in Scripture, *Assyria is the rod of My anger, and My indignation is a staff in their hand* (Isaiah 10:5). Thus He left their land in ruins and banished them among the nations. In effect, we might say, He cast the rebels into prison — the dungeon of dark exile.

Yet in His abounding mercy, the blessed Lord did not make an end of His people. His desire was only to subject some to the punishment they deserved: the true rebels, who had turned away from the path of the Torah and swayed and misled others to follow their ways of conduct. For them the sentence was death: They were all to descend into the dark of exile and never succeed in seeing the light of rescue and redemption.

Well, this is why the Almighty lets them enjoy their brief life on earth, in comfort and luxury. Soon, all too soon, comes the day of reckoning for them, when their life on earth ends and they find the punishment they deserve.

It is quite a different matter for righteous people of piety — those who remained loyal to God and His Torah in the depths of their heart, but were misled into following the paths of the wicked, when they took them away from the path of God. Now these people stay in the bitter exile, weeping and suffering, broken-hearted with regret and remorse over all the foolish and sinful things they did. These righteous people of piety will merit to be rescued from their dungeon of exile, and return to their original places of high rank. The land of their inheritance, once bestowed on our people as Heaven's gift, will be returned to them. And they will bask again in their original esteem and prosperity, as of old.

Consider then: In comparison with the great good fortune that is destined to come, of what significance are the suffering and troubles that afflict the righteous people of piety temporarily in their prison dungeon of today, until the time of their redemption?

98
TO KEEP FAITH WITH THE STEADY EMPLOYER

In every man's life there are different times and periods. At times he rises in fortune, and things go well with him; and at times he descends. Whenever a man goes through a difficult period, though, Satan the vile scoundrel goes to work on him and tries to turn his heart away from the good path of the Lord. 'Look', the evil impulse whispers, 'what are you going to gain from keeping the mitzvoth, the Almighty's commandments, so faithfully? Here you see how you haven't helped yourself one bit by taking this path. You are a poor man, with nothing to show for all your toil and labor and piety. If you would only listen to me, take my advice and follow my path, you would soon see yourself in a different kind of life. To put it simply: you would really live!'

Let us illustrate the matter with a parable:

A man met a good friend of his on the street, and saw that his friend looked completely downhearted and miserable. "What is the matter?" he asked. "Has something dreadful happened?"

"I have been out of work for weeks", his friend replied, "and my savings are almost gone. I just don't know what to do."

"Well", said the man, "if you want, you can come to work for me, and I will pay you a good salary."

"That would be wonderful", said his friend. "But please tell me: Will it be steady work?"

"I'm afraid it is not. I only need someone for a few months."

"In that case", said his friend, "I cannot accept your offer. I would rather wait a few more weeks, until my regular employer will have work for me again. Then I can go back to my old job. If I go to work for you for a few months, and then I go back to my regular employer, he will ask me where I was all the time; and when I tell him, he won't want to take me back. Then the result will be that for the sake of some temporary work I will lose my regular, steady employment. I would much rather remain out of work for another few weeks and suffer through this period, just as long as I can go back to steady work afterward."

The same holds true for the man we described above, at the beginning. At times it may happen that on account of a man's bad deeds, the Almighty turns His watchful care (as it were) away from him for a while. Then his sources of income close up, his health suffers, or other troubles gather and befall him. Immediately, the satanic evil impulse gets to work and tries to sway him toward some sinful deed. Then a man must bear in mind, above all else, that all these troubles are only temporary. Like a temporary loss of employment, they will pass. Finally, though, his virtue and merit will stand by him. His good deeds will be remembered, and his Divine Employer will return him to his "regular job", giving him his "salary" in full.

99
ALL GRAB EQUALLY

In Scripture we read, *sin crouches at the door* (Genesis 4:7). Now, why should it choose the term "sin", which denotes the lightest kind of wrongdoing, and not "iniquity" or "deliberate transgression", which mean more serious misdeeds?

This can be explained with a parable: A merchant once failed in his business activities and found himself bankrupt. The rumors of his situation reached his creditors soon enough, and they came, almost

like vultures, to his place of business and to his home, to seize whatever they could find.

Their claims were of varying sizes. Some were owed twenty thousand
dollars, some ten thousand, and some two thousand dollars. As they
milled about, seeking what they could take in partial payment for their
claims, one man arrived to join them in their "treasure hunt"; he too
was a creditor, he said. Well, the others asked, how much did the
bankrupt merchant owe him? A hundred dollars, he replied.

As they went about seizing and snatching what they could, they saw
the man who had arrived last, also going about and taking things. At
that the others turned on him in anger and tried to snatch away from
him whatever objects he had already gotten into his hands. "Just a
moment", said he. "What are you doing? I am also a creditor."

"Don't make us laugh", said the others. "This merchant owes you
a mere hundred dollars, and he owes us heavy thousands. How do you
compare yourself to us? We have so much greater rights than you to
anything in this place!"

"I will tell you", said the man. "If we were all sitting at a table
with the merchant, trying to collect from him what we could, you
would be perfectly right. Whatever money he would have, you would
be entitled to it far more than me. But now we are simply milling
around and seizing what we can. Then whatever anyone snatches is
his. In this we are all equal!"

As long as we are alive and everything goes along as usual, certainly
there is a difference between a person with a great debt of guilt toward
the blessed Lord, and one with a small debt of guilt, having done only
a few minor sins. For a major sin, bringing great guilt, there is major,
serious punishment. For a minor sin there is only light punishment.
Every debt must have its own proper payment.

"At the door" however (to go back to our opening verse from
Scripture), which means when a man dies and is at the door of the
grave — in a sense, he is like a merchant who has gone bankrupt,
whereupon the creditors come milling about, snatching, pulling and
seizing what they can, in an attempt to collect their debts. Similarly,

all the foul and evil deeds that the deceased man committed in his
lifetime come flocking about, to exact punishment. At such a time even
"sin", the lightest kind of misdeed, the very smallest "creditor", also
comes and tries to grasp what it can, to make the man pay with some
suffering for his misdeed. . . .

100
THE HAPPY DRUNKARDS

There are people in this world who live out their lives like the blind
who have never seen the light of day. Immersed and enmeshed in
their lowly appetites and earthly cravings, they do not even sense how
the forces of evil pull them deeper and deeper into the mire and quick-
sand of sin. Moreover, in their folly they think themselves happy and
fortunate. They are always full of gaiety and laughter, richly enjoying
their pleasure-laden and guilt-laden life.

They can be compared to a certain alcoholic who once became very
inebriated, and while under the influence he lost all his money. Finally
he even gave away the clothing he wore for a bottle of whiskey; and
then he was found lying in the mud, covered with filth and muck, but
otherwise unclothed and barefoot. Feeling completely happy, though,
as the alcohol did its work inside him, he clapped his hands for joy
and sang a lilting song. The poor addle-pated soul did not even know
how unfortunate he was. He was unable to grasp the miserable situation in which he wallowed. He had not the slightest idea that he was
without clothing, covered with filth, and completely penniless. He
would have to wait till the whiskey wore off and he sobered up. Then
his bleary, bloodshot eyes would glimpse reality; he would see just
where he was and in what condition; and he would understand what
had happened to him — and he would become a dejected, miserable
soul, broken by shame and anguish.

The same sort of thing is bound to happen to the people with earthly
cravings who pursue their pleasures. While they are immersed in their
sins, drunk from the sensual persuasions of the evil impulse that pulls
and pushes them toward perdition, they do not sense at all how they

are wasting their life on absolute nonsense, losing their share of life in the world-to-come — because they are in the process of losing the Divine image in which man was created.

Yet they are happy, celebrating and imagining that everything is wonderful for them.

Only when they reach the world of truth, the Hereafter, and they see the terrible fate awaiting them for all their evil actions in this world — only then will they sober up and understand that they have been wallowing in mire and muck all their life. Then their spirit will break and they will grieve in lament for their life that they wasted completely.

Alas, though, it will be too late then to do anything about it, and no remorse whatever will be of any use.

101
A PLACE TO COME HOME TO

One itinerant merchant made his living by riding to the large cities to buy his wares, after which he would make the rounds of the small villages and outlying rural areas to peddle and sell the items.

This was, however, no easy way for him to earn a living. Many itinerant merchants and traveling peddlers did this all week, riding around away from their homes, to make their sales. But they came home every Friday to spend the holy Sabbath at rest with their families. This poor Jew kept wandering about for weeks at a time, suffering all the discomforts of lonely travel, until he succeeded in selling his stock of goods. Only once a month or once in two months would he come home at last for a brief while.

By chance, some acquaintances came across him in the course of his traveling, and they saw that he was in a mood of deep sadness and melancholy. "What is the matter?" they asked him. "Has anything happened?"

"My dear wife, the companion of all my years, has died", he said. "Now I am quite alone, and I have no home any more, to come back to after all this wearying labor of mine."

"But why should it matter so much?" they asked him. "It cannot

be such a terrible blow to you. You have always been used to wandering around alone in any case. You were hardly home at all."

The peddler sighed and groaned in his heartbreaking grief: "How
can you compare one thing to the other? Till now, when I kept riding
around these villages far from home, I knocked about alone for long
stretches of time; but I knew that at the end of it all there was a home
waiting for me. At the end of my wandering I would return for a
while. I would sit at my own table and sleep restfully in my bed. Now,
with my dear wife gone, I have nothing left. Every time I think that
there is no longer any home for me to return to, any place that I will
be able to call my own dwelling, all the afflictions of this wandering
life of mine become seven times as hard to bear."

This explains the difference between the righteous men of piety and
the wicked men of evil. This world is only an entrance-hall, leading
to a splendid mansion in the Hereafter. All who inhabit this earth
wander and move about like itinerant peddlers, bearing the hardships.
Only, the righteous men of piety live with the hope that after all the
afflictions of being tossed about on this earth, after they have "sold"
their little stock of "merchandise" in this world, they will receive in
payment a share of life in the world-to-come. Then they will have a
dwelling, a home of their own, to which they can go and rest: an abode
of endless peace. Knowing this, they can bear the distress and troubles
of their wandering on earth. It does not seem that painful any more.

The wicked, however, live without this hope. They have no home
waiting for them when they return from making the rounds on their
journey through life. Then certainly whatever they suffer on this earth,
from being tossed about by the hardships of life, must be seven times
as difficult for them to bear. For when it will all be over, no restful
home awaits them in the Hereafter.

102

THE EFFECT OF UNPAID DEBTS

It is a basic teaching in Jewish mysticism that for every single penny
which a man remains owing when he leaves this world, he has to be

reincarnated (Heaven spare us). He must return again to this abased world; he must be born into it once more, so that he can pay back what he owes.

Let no one take this matter of reincarnation lightly, however. To have to be born again is a hard and frightful fate. To understand it properly, let us explain with a parable:

A man once failed in his business and found himself without any way of earning a living. With no choice, he left his wife and children and set off for a distant country, on a journey of thousands of miles over land and sea. In that country, where he stayed many years, he was able to support himself by dint of hard labor and great toil. Happiness, though, he did not find. He remained sad and bitter at the turn in his fortunes.

In the course of time, however, he went into business in that faraway land, and found himself successful. It took only a short while for him to become a rich man. Then he sent off a letter to his family, to tell them the news of his success, and of his plans to leave the country shortly and return home. He warned his family, however, not to expect him too soon. It would take him all of seven months till he could be with them again.

When his letter arrived, it made his wife and children happy beyond all description. At last, they felt, fortune was smiling on them.

Before the man actually left his new country to return home, a good friend gave him some advice: "Since you are leaving permanently and you don't plan to return, look over your accounts very carefully and make sure you don't owe anyone anything. If you leave with debts, you may have a lot of trouble. We have a powerful king, and he may send police officers to bring you back here."

The man laughed. He had no large, serious debts. If he still owed some small amounts here and there, for some unpaid bills that he could not remember, he could hardly imagine the king ordering him brought back over a matter of a few pennies. He refused to take his friend's advice seriously, and set off for home.

In the course of the journey he wrote his family exactly when he would be arriving. On the expected day his wife and children went out to the port and waited impatiently for the ship to dock. It was many long years since they had seen him last. Finally the ship landed and they saw the man coming toward them.

What was this, however? Before he could pass through the gate and join them, they saw him taken aside by the seaport police. Then they saw him in earnest request, as he pleaded with the police to let him see his family at least for a short while before they sent him back. It was so many years since he had seen his wife and children.

"We would certainly like to let you go into the city for a while", the seaport police replied. "We understand. But what can we do? Here we have an official order from the country where you lived till now: It says that you owe someone there a sum of money, and he demands payment. There is no way for you to pay it here, so we must send you back. After you clear up this matter you can return."

The man fell to the policemen's feet and begged and sobbed piteously: "It is ten years since I've seen my wife and children. Please let me go to them for an hour. Then I will go back to that country. Just let me go to them. Here: I will pay the debt *twice* over. Here is my money: take it. Only let me go now to my home!"

"What is the good of paying *us* twice what you owe someone over there? We have no way of getting your money to him."

"Then at least let me stay here a month with my family. Afterward I will board a ship and travel back there. Are you really going to refuse to let me even see my family after I have been away for ten years and have journeyed seven long months to see them?"

Plead and beg as he would, it was all in vain, however. "Then at least", he finally asked, "let me see them from afar. Let me look at my wife and children without talking to them."

To this the police consented: "Very well. You may look at them, and then you will board ship to start your journey back."

For a few moments his wife and children were overjoyed. They saw the gate opening and the man walking toward them, and they thought he had been released. Then they realized, to their dismay, that the police remained firmly at his side, and at a certain point he had to stop, being allowed to go no further. His family and he looked at each other for a few long moments; then he was taken back and they saw him no more.

It needs no great effort to imagine the man's feelings when he found himself on board ship, bound for the country he had left some seven months before. Nor can any doubt remain whether he wished he had listened to his friend in that country and paid off *all* his debts before he left.

It is the very same with a man's way in the world. How much toil he must bear in this lowly world, how much suffering he must undergo, till he can reach the world of truth, the Hereafter, his place of origin, where his true eternal home is to be found, amid his close kin and family of old. After so many years of adversity and difficulty, after the discomfort and pain of the long journey, he reaches the destination, for which he has yearned so very long. And what does he find? He must return to this vile valley, this pitiful world on earth — all on account of a few pennies that he remained owing. . . .

Is it not worth making sure, then, that no debts remain?

103

THEY HAD ONLY THEMSELVES TO BLAME

Our Sages teach: The countenance of Moses was like the face of the sun; the countenance of Joshua, like the face of the moon. The elders of that generation said, "Woe for that shame, woe for that disgrace" (Talmud, Bava Bathra 75a).

This seems very puzzling. Why the mention of shame and disgrace? Did they mean that because Joshua's countenance was only like the face of the moon, it was a reason for shame and disgrace? Yet Joshua too attained a high level spiritually, as Scripture says, *Joshua . . . was full of the spirit of wisdom,* etc. (Deuteronomy 34:9).

We can explain it, however, with a story: A certain man heard that in one country overseas, very precious diamonds had been discovered. Whoever wanted could come and mine them, and he was sure to make a fortune. He decided to travel out there, but thought it best to gather a staff of workers to come with him. So he went to several friends

and told them of the bright prospects in the far-off land, and invited
them to travel out with him. They all refused, however, feeling that
it was too far away, out in the middle of nowhere, and the long sea
voyage would be too much for them. Only one proved to be an exception to the rule: he agreed to come along.

A few years later the two returned, carrying a valuable cache of
rare diamonds in their baggage. And as they began selling the precious
stones to dealers, they became rich overnight. When their friends saw
this, they turned green with envy, suffering the pangs of deep regret
that they had not agreed to go along with the two on the sea voyage.
They too could have become wealthy so easily.

These are the kind of pangs of regret that the elders of that generation
suffered, long ago. Joshua had been one of them, no more and no less.
They had been his equals. Yet he alone, and not they, rose to eminence
and distinction by becoming Moses' successor, because he had always
been with Moses, the master instructor of all Israel, serving him and
attending upon him. So they suffered the anguish of regret, crying,
"Woe, woe! We also had the right and the opportunity to serve Moses
and attend upon him. We too could thus have risen to this great level,
to attain the gifts of prophecy and complete wisdom, just as Joshua
did. If we failed to do so, we have only ourselves to blame. Woe for
the shame of it, woe for the disgrace!"

104
PLANNING THE HOME

As a rule, when a man wants to build a home, he does not design it
and draw up the plans, but hires a reliable architect. According to the
architect's conception and detailed plans, builders go ahead and con-
struct the house. It is he who places the anteroom, the living room,
and so forth, determining also the exact size of every room.

A rich man once engaged an architect to plan his home, having
bought a plot of land for it. As best he could, he tried to make his
wishes clear about the various rooms, so that the architect could take
his wishes into account in drawing the plans. "You understand", he

said, "I want a very large and impressive living room. Of course, the anteroom must also be of a respectable size."

The architect considered the size of the ground for the home, and reported back, "I am afraid you cannot have everything you want. If the living room is to be an impressive size, really spacious, then you can have only a small anteroom. If you want a good-sized anteroom, we will have to reduce the size of the living room. You have to decide which you prefer. . . . If you want my advice, though, you will make the living room large and stately, and leave the anteroom small. This is what people generally do in a case like this. The living room is the important part of the house — the central feature. It should be as handsome as you can make it. On the other hand, if you do it the other way — reduce the living room for the sake of a handsome anteroom — it will look ridiculous. People will laugh at you, wondering at what you have gone and done. After all, the anteroom is only for people to pass through when they arrive. The living room is where they stay during their visit. That is the room they really see and remember. We should put our best efforts into that."

During our stay on earth we build a home for ourselves in the world-to-come. As our Sages teach in *Midrash Mishley,* "Whoever acquires words of Torah, acquires a house in the world-to-come." What do we do, though? We invest our time, our effort and energy, to build a larger and fancier anteroom or entrance-hall. Our Sages teach that this world of ours is like an anteroom to the world-to-come. All we do to improve our life in this world, to build a bigger, better, fancier home — amounts to enlarging and improving the anteroom, at the expense of the living room: the true home where we live for all time.

Is that a wise and sensible approach to take?

105
UNREALIZED OPPORTUNITIES

When a poor man lives on charity, how much money can he be expected to have? Probably a handful of pennies; perhaps a few nickels and dimes; maybe a few dollars. There have been many indigent souls who never saw twenty dollars at any one time in their life. They would gather pennies each day, till they had enough for their simple needs. If a poor man like that ever found a hundred-dollar bill, he might never realize what a valuable piece of paper it was, never having seen the like of it and not understanding what the words and numbers on it mean. Very possibly, as he saw it lying on the street, he might not even trouble himself to bend down and pick it up, thinking it only some fancy, decorated piece of paper.

Believe it or not, we — poor in understanding — can be likened to such a penniless beggar.

The blessed Lord gave us a wonderful gift: the holy Torah with its 613 mitzvoth. No eye but His alone (if we may so speak) has ever beheld the reward given for every mitzvah that is observed. Not all the riches in the world can compare to the compensation given eventually for even the slightest mitzvah that was kept.

Then our simple reason should tell us that having received the Torah, we ought to run after every single mitzvah, seeking it out like valuable treasure, to observe it with our very life, so as to earn the fabulous reward for it. The sad truth is, however, that very few people will literally run after an opportunity to do any and every mitzvah that they can. Persons generally feel themselves extremely rich spiritually, when they have observed even one mitzvah of the Torah.

Why is it so? — because we simply do not realize what tremendous wealth each and every mitzvah can bring us. We are so impoverished in our understanding that we are content to live (spiritually) on a few pennies every day, that we gather like a beggar. We don't even have the ability to recognize the difference between miserable pennies — which, even if we gather a whole mound of them, will never add up to any great value — and a genuine fortune in bills of large denomination, such as hundred-dollar bills. So it makes no impression on us to learn that such fabulous amounts of money (so to speak) await us in spiritual reward constantly, every hour, for mitzvoth waiting to be observed. We have only to reach out and earn them, to live a blessed, fortunate life in this world and in the next.

VII: THE EVIL INCLINATION

106
THE BALANCE OF WEALTH

Many years ago there was a certain young adult who spent his time studying at the yeshivah of the Ḥafetz Ḥayyim in Radun. Possessed of Talmudic knowledge, he was an excellent scholar and a person of great piety. Yet he suffered from dire poverty. Often he would complain to the Ḥafetz Ḥayyim about his bitter lot in life; and he would beg the pious sage to pray for him, that Heaven should take pity on him and release him from the terrible constraint of poverty. He gave the Ḥafetz Ḥayyim his word that when the good Lord would help him rise to affluence, he would give a tenth of his wealth every year to charity, even if it cost him thousands.

"Yet who am I, what am I", the pious sage retorted, "that you ask this of me? You have to pray directly to the blessed Lord, with all your heart, to plead with Him for mercy. And if your prayer is accepted, Heaven's rescuing help will come and your wish will be granted you. I must warn you, however, that you have to keep the promise you have made. Woe to anyone who treats lightly the kind of obligation that you have now undertaken. Once you have any kind of respectable income, you *must* give a tenth to charity."

Not too long afterward, the young man found an opportunity to go into business. The Almighty blessed his efforts, and in the course of a few years he became so successful that he received a special permit from the government of the Russian czar to live in Moscow — a privilege that only the wealthiest among the Jews could ever hope to receive.

The only trouble was that once he became a man of wealth, he completely forgot the promise he had made to the Ḥafetz Ḥayyim. He became a hard, tight-fisted man, and not a penny would he give to charity.

The Ḥafetz Ḥayyim kept himself informed of the man's progress, and knew all about him. Never once, though, would he mention him when speaking to mutual friends.

One day the pious sage had to go to Moscow for the sake of his yeshivah. When he arrived in the Russian capital, the prominent Jews of the city came to his hotel room, to welcome him with honor; and among them the pious sage saw his former pupil, who had risen from grinding poverty to great wealth, and had become a tight-fisted miser in the process. As the man came forward to greet the sage, his face was wreathed in smiles. He was genuinely happy to see his former instructor in Torah. The gathered people spoke a while with the Ḥafetz Ḥayyim, then took their leave and departed. His former student, however, stayed behind in the sage's hotel room.

When the two were alone, this former student of his suddenly burst into tears. "Dear rabbi", he cried, "help me. I have a serious sickness; and what makes it worse is that I know what the illness is, and I cannot do anything about it."

"Why, what is this illness of yours? What is the trouble?"

"My hands are shut tight, as if under lock and key. I cannot open them. I cannot bring myself to give a penny to charity. My heart has become hard as a rock. Do you think I have forgotten? I remember the promise I made when I was suffering from miserable poverty and I asked you to pray for me. I promised to give away a tenth of my income. Yet what am I to do? I have no control over my heart and hands. Satan seems to be in firm control, and he won't let me give any charity. Tell me, dear rabbi: why has this happened to me?"

The Ḥafetz Ḥayyim patted him on the shoulder and smiled. "Here", he said, "let me tell you a story." And this is what he told:

On the day before a *yom tov*, a Jewish farmer came into the city to buy what he needed for the festival. He went to the store where he usually made his purchases, and asked for three dollars' worth of flour.

"Do me a favor", said the storekeeper. "Take an empty bag from there and put it here on the balance-scale. Take the scoop and pour in as much flour as you need, from the big sack over there. Then I will put the weights on the other pan of the scale and see how much flour you have."

Happy at the thought that he was free to take the flour by himself, the farmer took a large bag and filled it to the top. The storekeeper, as it seemed to him, paid no attention. When he had everything else that he needed and was ready to leave, he took the bag of flour and held out three dollars.

"Just a moment", said the storekeeper. "You took a large bag and filled it mighty full. That is not three dollars' worth but ten dollars' worth. You are not going to give me just three dollars for a large bag of flour like that!"

"But I asked you for three dollars' worth", the farmer protested, "and you told me to fill the bag myself. When I filled it you did not say a word. So I thought that whatever amount I took, it would cost me three dollars. Why do you come and ask for ten dollars now?"

"Well, when I saw you take that large bag and fill it up, I thought you had changed your mind and decided to take more than you planned. I didn't know anything. I just stood at the side and put weights on the scale till they balanced your flour. Why — did you think you could just keep pouring and pouring, and it would still weigh the same?"

"This", the Ḥafetz Ḥayyim continued, "is what happened to you. When you were as poor as a mouse, and you spent your time studying Torah and keeping the mitzvoth, you had an evil inclination to fit your income and your situation. You had no trouble being devout and promising to give a tenth of your income to charity. Did you think you could just have Heaven pour down its blessing of wealth on you, on your side of the balance-scale, and the weights on the other side — the satanic evil inclination — would remain just the same?

"That, my friend, is a sad mistake on your part. The more you gain in material wealth from Heaven's beneficence, on the balance-scale of your spirit, the heavier the weights become on the other side. A man has to know the price he will have to pay at the end, for all that pours into his bag of possessions."

107

"IF I WERE IN HIS PLACE"

A man who loved whiskey took so much of it that he went out into the street thoroughly inebriated. As he walked, he managed to stay on his feet only with the greatest difficulty, as he bobbed and weaved. Finally the effort became too much for him, and he fell flat on his face, stretched out from head to toe in a pile of garbage and filth. From this vantage point he looked out at life, cursing, calumniating and abusing everyone and everything, in the best tradition of veteran drunkards.

As might be expected, children of various sizes and idlers with nothing better to do gathered around him to mock, make comments, and throw rotten vegetables at the victim of the bottle.

One man who thought himself particularly intelligent happened by, and he stopped to regard the drunkard thoughtfully. "It serves you right", he said. "You deserve to lie in the filth and muck like that, you poor fool. You just don't know how to hold your liquor. You take three or four drinks, and you don't know how to behave anymore. If I were in your place, I would never come to this. Give me three, four quarts of the stuff, and I'll still walk down the street cool as a cucumber. You won't catch *me* rolling in the garbage like that, for every passerby to laugh at me!"

Two persons standing nearby smiled and winked to each other. They remembered this man who was talking now. A week or two before, he had been just as thoroughly filled with whiskey, and had behaved not a whit better.

There are people who speak out against rich and wealthy Jews who refuse to give properly to charity. "Just look at those misers", such people say. "If we had their money, we would know how to use it so that the treasuries of charity would fill up a bit."

They are blissfully unaware that if they became rich, they would probably be worse. Their hearts would become hard as stone, and they would be no better than anyone else. They simply do not realize that wealth is a kind of intoxication, having an effect like alcohol.

108

HOW TO GET STUCK IN THE MUD

In a certain small town there was a fool, who did not have all his wits about him, whom everyone knew. One day, one of the town's so-called jesters, known for his practical jokes, decided to have some fun at the fool's expense. He would get the poor fellow out to the edge of town, and get him into a large mud puddle that was there, so that everyone could come and see, and have a good laugh. That was the jokester's idea of great humor.

What did he do? He went to the witless fool and gave him all kinds of sweets and goodies, till the poor fellow thought the jokester was his true friend. Then the jokester said, "Come: let us take a walk to the edge of town." Suspecting nothing, the poor fool agreed; and the two set off. It would take them an hour or two to reach the mud puddle; and to make sure the simpleton would not grow peevish and change his mind and turn back, the man kept plying him with sweet candies and sweet words, till the sun set and evening came on.

Now the jokester pretended that he wanted to reveal a deep dark secret to the poor fellow. He whispered in his ear, "I am going to tell you a great secret; but first you must promise me that it will remain just between us: You won't tell it to anyone else." Solemnly the simpleton gave him his hand and promised.

"Now", said the jokester, "do you know that here at the edge of town, not far from where we are standing, there is a great puddle of mud?"

"Oh yes", said the simpleton. "I even heard that it is very deep, and if anyone falls in he is liable to drown." There was a note of fear in his voice.

"And I tell you not to believe those silly stories. There is mud only over a narrow strip of land, and it is quite shallow. It is not deep at all. And beyond it a great treasure is buried. Long ago there was a fierce battle between two enemy armies on that spot. The side that was attacked buried the treasure there in a great hurry, before the other side might have a chance to find it. The other side won the battle — and the fabulous treasure was left there. Come, let us go in together.

We will go across the mud, dig up the treasure, and divide it equally between us."

The fool was persuaded. Believing and trusting the jokester, he went with him happily, and eagerly jumped into the mud puddle. The jokester, of course, made sure to stay on dry ground. The bewildered simpleton now found himself in mud up to his hips, and with every movement he made he only sank deeper. To his utter dismay, he saw his supposed friend walking away and laughing out loud.

"Help!" cried the simpleton. "Save me! I'm drowning! It will soon be up to my neck! I don't care about any treasure. Only come and save me."

The jokester paid no attention to his cries but kept walking swiftly away, laughing softly to himself: "Save you, my fine-feathered friend? Oh no; not much chance of that. It cost me quite a bit of money for all those sweets and goodies I needed to get you to come out here with me. It cost me hours of time and patience and trouble till I succeeded in getting you there — just where I wanted you: right in the mud. Now you want me to come and pull you out? You have a fat chance of that. I am going to call all the people of the town to come and enjoy the spectacle. Let them see just how big a baboon you are. This is going to be rich. I am going to enjoy this more than anything in years. My plan has worked out just perfectly!"

What is the moral of the story? It applies to a man and his satanic evil inclination.

When the evil impulse goes to work on a person, to tempt him into committing a sin and thus drag him into a mud puddle of guilt — it gives him "lovely little gifts" of "sweets and goodies" that draw his heart. The satanic force of persuasion always has plenty of "goodies" and tempting things for those whom it wants to swerve from the path of decency; and it promises them untold treasure of every kind of wonder. "Come, come", it whispers. "There is only a narrow, shallow stretch of mud to cross . . . and then *treasure*!"

Once a man has yielded to temptation, however, and listened to his evil impulse — and he thus finds himself sunk in the mud — the satanic tempter and persuader goes off on his way, his mouth filled with laughter at the stupidity of his victim. The poor man remains stuck in the mud, to face the music alone.

109
THE TECHNIQUE OF THE DEVIL

Do you want to know how Satan does his work — this vile scoundrel who, as the Talmud (Bava Bathra 16) says, "goes down and misleads, then goes up and brings accusations"? Let me explain with a parable:

A man learned that someone whom he hated bitterly had been hired as chief accountant for the business affairs of a very wealthy person, at a most ample salary. The news made the man furious. How did this person, whom he detested so thoroughly, ever manage to secure such a high, respectable position at such a good salary?

Unable to keep still, he went to the wealthy man and said, "I have been told that you own a large courtyard which is just standing idle. It is not being used for anything, and does not bring you any income. It has occurred to me that if you were to put an energetic and trustworthy man in charge of it, he could find ways of putting it to use so that it would bring you a fine monthly income. And I can suggest exactly the right man for the job: So-and-so, who is now in your employ as your chief accountant. I know the man, and I can tell you that he has just the qualifications for this task. He is reliable and resourceful."

This advice made a deep impression on the rich man, and he decided to act on it. He took his chief accountant away from his regular work and put him in charge of the empty, unused lot, with orders to find ways of making it profitable. Since this was not as respectable and estimable a position as that of chief accountant, he reduced the man's salary considerably.

To this accountant it was a hard blow. Yet what could he do? If this was his employer's wish, he had no choice but to accept it.

In a while the other man, who had persuaded the rich businessman to put the chief accountant into the new position, thought the matter over. "What have I gone and done?" he asked himself. "By my efforts this person whom I hate now has a good job at quite a decent salary. That is more than he deserves!''

Back he went to the rich businessman, and put his tongue to work again. This time he blackened the reputation of the other person in every way that he could. He slandered him and denounced him, till at last the wealthy businessman decided it would be best to dismiss his employee altogether.

This is exactly how the satanic evil inclination works, when it comes to tempt and drive us away from the path of the Torah.

When it sees a Jew in reverent fear of Heaven, keeping the Torah and the mitzvoth, it becomes riled up and indignant, knowing how great a reward in the Hereafter the man will earn. So it comes and persuades him that this "business" is not for him at all. It is not worth his while, it tells him. What should he do instead? There is a "court-yard" — this world of ours — from which he has not yet had any true benefit and pleasure. So, it beguiles him into thinking, it would be worth his while to devote himself particularly to the courtyard, and make that his business.

The credulous Jew is persuaded, and gets himself involved in matters and pleasures of this world. Then the satanic evil inclination takes a new look at the situation and sees that even this is too good for him. Satan begrudges him even the bit of pleasure and contentment that the man may find in this world. Without delay he goes up to heaven and brings an accusation against the man: "Just see what he is doing with the money he was given. He is as full of sins as a pomegranate is full of pits. He does not study the Torah. He does not keep the mitz-voth." And so the satanic accuser continues, on and on, till he drives the poor man out of this world.

110
THE DIVISIONS OF OUR ARMY

A man once came to the Ḥafetz Ḥayyim and asked, "What is the reason for the different arrangements of the prayers among the Jewish people? Why is there an Ashkenaz prayer-book, and a Sefard prayer-book? What need is there for both? And even among the *hassidim*, who use the Sefard rite, why are there different ways of praying? Some sway in fervor and enthusiasm, shouting, singing and dancing about. Others whisper in devotion and concentration; and so on. Would it not be much better if all the Jews used one system of prayer — one text and one way of worshipping?"

"Do you know?" replied the Ḥafetz Ḥayyim. "You could ask the very same kind of question of the Russian czar: 'Your majesty, why in the world do you need so many different kinds of soldiers and army divisions? Why do you have to have infantry and cavalry, artillery and seamen, border patrols and state police, and so on? Would it not be better if you made one standard kind of soldier out of them all, outfitted with the same kind of weapons and equipment, led by one commanding officer? It would simplify matters so much for your government. It would remove so many problems and headaches.'

"What is the answer, though? Every person with sense knows that each kind of army unit has a different task and a separate purpose, which it alone can do. The basic general purpose of an army is to defeat the enemy in case of war. But for this single goal they devise different ways and means. So by experiment and experience they found that what an infantryman can do, a cavalryman cannot, and so vice-versa. The infantry can fight well at close range, in face-to-face combat. Cavalry can move swiftly, to flee the enemy when necessary, or to pursue it at great speed. The artillery divisions, manning their cannon and heavy guns, can strike deadly blows at the enemy from afar — which no other divisions can do. Even the buglers and trumpeters, and the fife-and-drum corps, who can do no actual fighting, serve a necessary purpose: They raise the spirits of the soldiers and rouse them to fight.

"Well, in our observance of our religion, all our activities are one constant, concerted war against the element of evil: Satan, the tempter who seeks to mislead us. So we look and search for stratagems and techniques to be able to prevail against him and vanquish him. For this basic purpose, we have different kinds of fighting units in our army: infantry, cavalry and artillery. Each kind is of great importance for its particular purpose. Each one fights the enemy in its way, with its own particular weapons. Each helps achieve victory by its own approach, carrying out tasks which the other units cannot do.

"Thus one type scores a victory by studying Torah; another, by the power of prayer; a third, by singing melodies of religious devotion; and so on. The main thing is that every group, every army unit of ours, should know that our one and only purpose is to battle the evil impulse and prevail against it!"

111
THE RESULT OF RELYING ON THE HORSE

A merchant had to take a trip to another city, in order to attend to business matters. His affairs in that city finished, he hired the driver of a horse-and-wagon to take him home.

Before they set off on the journey, the merchant told the driver, "Look, my dear man: I have just eaten a very good lunch, with a splendid bottle or two of a fragrant wine. I am quite certainly going to drowse off on the way and have a good nap. That means that you alone will have to keep a good eye on the horse and make sure it doesn't go off the road and throw the whole wagon into a ditch. Be very careful that *you* do not go to sleep. Do you hear?" The wagon-driver promised to keep awake.

The wagon hardly started to roll along the road, before the merchant was fast asleep, snoring gently, lulled by the steady clack of the wheels and the horse's hooves. The driver, remembering his promise, did his best to remain alert and handle the reins properly. Alas, though, he too had just eaten a rather heavy lunch, before setting off on the journey. For a while he made a strong effort and resisted the encroaching drowsiness. Then it all became too much for him. He gave up the struggle, and his eyelids closed to let him into blissful slumber. The reins slipped from his hands, and the horse trotted along briskly on its own initiative.

Feeling no restraint from reins or bridle, the animal lifted up its eyes from the road and saw some lovely pasture off at the side — tender luxuriant grass. Without a second thought, the creature headed for the grass. Behind it, of course, came the wagon. It went off the road and into the ditch, turning over on its side and throwing its two sleeping passengers into the ditch filled with mud. The merchant was jolted awake, and severely bruised into the bargain.

As he sat up and looked about, he understood what had happened. The horse grazing happily in the grass told its own story. He turned on the stupefied driver and poured out his wrath on him: "You absolute idiot! I warned you not to fall asleep and let go of the reins. I warned you not to let the horse run on its own. I knew it would lead us right into disaster. Why didn't you listen to me? I may have broken a bone. It is painful for me to move!"

"Just a moment", the driver retorted. "Are you accusing me of being responsible for your injuries? That is not fair. At first I held the reins perfectly. But I know my horse is an intelligent animal, and it always behaves properly. So I was sure I could depend on it to follow the road very well. Then by accident — I couldn't help it — I dozed off a bit. How was I to know that the horse would suddenly go off the road? You cannot really blame me for that."

"Oh no?" the merchant shouted. "You are a bigger fool than I thought. You seem to be trying to tell me that I ought to take the horse to court and sue *it* for damages. You are so disappointed in this 'intelligent' animal of yours. You had a high opinion of it, you tell me; so you thought you could depend on it. Don't you know that a horse is just a horse, ever and always? You cannot rely on its brains for anything more. Unfortunately, you did — and now you see the result."

As we know, every human being has an intelligent self and an animal self. Whenever a person does not keep a suitable hold on the reins of self-control, whenever he stops watching his animal self to keep it on the straight and proper path — he faces the danger that it will crave the sweet tender pasture at the side of the road, whereupon it will veer sharply off, overturning the wagon completely. The animal self may be very cultured and intelligent in its way, but despite everything it is still an animal.

This is why a man must take care constantly to make sure that the intelligent self, informed by Torah and reason, keeps the reins firmly in hand and watches the animal self well, so that it will not swerve from the good and decent path and lead the wagon right into the ditch. Should anything like this happen, it will be ridiculous to argue afterward in self-defense, "It was the animal's fault. *It* went off the road..." A careful driver of the vehicle of the self will not doze off for even a minute, to give the animal element a chance to go off gallivanting on its own.

112
WHEN IT PAYS TO PAY NO ATTENTION

In the Eastern Europe of an earlier time, when a fledgling merchant came down to the market for the first time, with goods to sell, the veteran traders and merchants used to welcome him with jeering laughter and mockery: "Just look at that", they would say. "We have trouble enough with us older dealers here, and you come along to join the ranks? Couldn't you find any better way of earning a living? You would do well to look for another occupation. You won't find much glory on this road."

Of course, if the newcomer was intelligent and clever, he would pay no attention to the laughter and the scornful words. He would simply continue on his own way. At first, he would find things hard. He would need some painful education in the school of experience. Ultimately, however, he would find the smiling face of success, and would see the blessing of Divine providence in his labors. Once he reached this stage, he could turn on the veteran traders and dealers who had mocked him, and laugh at them, saying, "Had I listened to you, I would have stayed poor all my life."

In the same way, there is no need for a man to pay any attention to those who may scorn and mock him for taking the path of the Torah and keeping its mitzvoth, in reverent fear of the Almighty's word. This world of ours is a kind of marketplace; whoever studies the Torah here and observes its mitzvoth will find that he is in a good business venture indeed, spiritually: great reward awaits him in the world-to-come. Once he gets there, it is he who will be able to laugh and give a sharp retort to those who jeered at him, paying them back in good measure for all their derision.

113
THE PERSISTENCE OF THE FLY

What made the Sages teach (Talmud, B'rachoth 61) that "the evil inclination is comparable to a fly"? Why did they choose particularly that small, disgusting creature as a simile for the evil impulse in the human being?

Well, we know that all creatures in the world can generally be driven away by fear. They only have to be frightened off once, twice or three times, and they will stop troubling a person. Not so the fly, however. Once it comes to trouble someone, it swarms and buzzes around him ceaselessly. No matter how many times it is frightened off, it comes back and bothers you again, without any let-up. It will give you no peace — until you destroy it.

The same is true of the evil inclination: It does not grow ashamed or frightened by anything in the world. However much you try to drive it away and be rid of it, it comes right back to you. Hurl it out on one path, and on seven paths it will return to you. There is no way to get rid of it. It must be battled and struggled against, till we prevail against it.

VIII: MISCELLANY

114
THE NEED TO PREPARE

If a man wishes to give a festive meal in his home for his family, kin and dear friends, he begins making his preparations a good number of days or even weeks before; and when the invited people appear on the appointed day, they find the tables tastefully set. The food is all prepared. The bottled beverages are set out on the tables. And the host himself stands in the doorway, handsomely dressed, all ready to receive his guests.

What would the invited guests say, though, if they came at the proper time and found nothing whatever ready for the feast: the tables bare, the food uncooked, the bottled beverages not yet arrived — and the host moving about in ordinary weekday clothes? It is easy to imagine the anger and dismay of the invited people. They would resent their host for having made the whole thing one great matter of embarrassment, or perhaps one enormous insult to them all.

After all, he invited them personally. He was quite specific about the day and the hour. Then why did he do nothing about it all the time till now? Did he expect to begin making all the preparations now, with all the guests standing about? He only proved himself a liar, who was ready to make fools of others.

Several times a day we pray that the blessed Lord should send us Elijah the prophet to bring us the happy news of the advent of our righteous Messiah, after which the holy Temple will be rebuilt and the service of sacrifices and offerings will be renewed. Fine! Yet we on our part are doing nothing to prepare for that day when Elijah will appear. We are not learning the laws of the offerings and the holy Temple service. We are not preparing the kohanim (the descendants of Aaron) to know how to perform the service; and without them no Divine service can even be started at the holy Temple.

In effect, then, when we pray for Elijah the prophet to come, we prove ourselves liars, who are ready to make fools of others. Do we expect to win Heaven's favor in this way?

What remains then to be done? Every Jew who is able, especially a kohen, has a duty to learn the subject of holy Temple offerings and the Divine service involved in dealing with them. Then, when Elijah the prophet comes to bring the news of the advent of our righteous Messiah, we will be able to welcome him properly.

115

LIVING HIGH OR LOW

In our so-called "modern" world it seems to be the accepted goal of life to succeed in making money and yet more money. All effort and energy, all planning and thought seems concentrated on this one purpose.

In his feverish pursuit of money, though, a person would do well to stop and reflect that he can be compared to a certain nobleman of an earlier age, who owned vast estates. The man was famous in his time as one of the very richest in the land. Having limitless wealth, he grew accustomed to eating expensive delicacies and drinking only the finest liquors; and in general he indulged himself in all kinds of sensual pleasures. When he ate his fabulous meals of exotic and exquisite dishes, musicians would play sweet music at his table.

In short, he denied himself nothing. Every wish of his became a demand and a command. Servants were always about, ready to do his bidding.

So beguiled was he, however, by all his pleasure and self-indulgence that his mind became addled. Driven by some foolish or lunatic urge, he turned traitor against his native land and became helpful to his country's bitterest enemy.

His treachery was soon discovered, though. He was arrested, brought to trial, and found guilty. Then the court pronounced sentence: He was to be taken to the top of a high tower built on a cliff, at whose feet yawned a deep abyss. There he was to live, on the rather small roof of the tower, that had no proper parapet or railing. But he was to be allowed to live in his usual style. At the edge of the roof, over-looking the abyss below, he was to be given the sumptuous meals and superb liquors to which he was accustomed. Musicians were to be brought to play for him, as they did in his home; and so was he to be given all his usual pleasures and delights — whatever he wished. He was to be denied nothing that his heart might desire — until the day that old age brought his life to an end.

Somehow, though, there was no more pleasure left in anything for the man. The most delicious food seemed without taste now. The rarest wines brought him no cheer. He listened to the sweetest music, and it had no effect. Always before his eyes was the abyss awaiting him beyond the edge of the tower's roof. Given a choice, he would dearly wish to give up all the pleasure and luxury and self-indulgence, and go live in a miserable little shepherd's hut, to subsist there on a little bread and water, as long as he would not see that awful abyss before him every time he turned around, a hundred times a day....

Consider now a person rushing madly through life to gather money and become rich (and if already rich, to become richer). Is he not really in the same situation? Amassing his wealth, he learns to live like the rich. He can indulge himself and his family in pleasures and delights. Luxuries become customary, and then necessary.

Yet does not such man really live on the unguarded roof of a tower, beside an abyss? The day can come when one impulsive or unwise action of his, or one unforeseen turn of events, can hurl him from the tower of wealth into the abyss of poverty and want. How will he ever survive that? How can he adjust to living penniless? How can he learn to eke out an existence, to live from hand to mouth, when he has grown accustomed to the sweet, luxurious life of plenty in the affluence of success?

Behind his rich life of pleasure, every wealthy man lives haunted, somewhere in the recesses of his awareness, by the specter of a dis-astrous turn in his fortunes, a plunge into the abyss of poverty. It is far, far better then to live on a simple, modest scale, with inner peace — without the anxiety about falling from the heights to the depths.

116
YOU CAN GET USED TO IT, UNFORTUNATELY

A man who owned a perfume shop, where he manufactured and sold his bottles of scent and ointments, was quite content with his life, till a tanner came and opened a leather shop right next to him. From the tanner's shop, where the man always treated animal skins to produce the leather that he sold, a foul odor always came, which contrasted all too sharply with the fragrance and atmosphere of the perfume shop. This made the perfumer resent the tanner. He could not forgive the man for having opened his shop right next door. And for this reason he would never speak to the man.

Unfortunately, though, fate turned against the perfumer. The competition of other perfume shops in the city was too strong, and he had to give up his store. He went everywhere looking for employment, trying to find some way to earn a living, but with no success. Finally the tanner, his former neighbor, met him on the street; and he invited the perfumer to become his partner. His business was growing, and it was too much for him to manage alone.

At first the perfumer could not even bear to think of it. Even from afar he could not tolerate the odor of the leather being tanned. How could he possibly make that his occupation? His savings came to an end, however, and he saw his family facing actual hunger. With no choice left, he went to the leather shop and accepted the man's offer.

During his first day in the place, he was forced to keep a cloth tied over his nose, so that the odor should not be so penetrating and sickening. He suffered, as it was all he could do to keep from feeling ill. Only by the strongest efforts was he able to last through the day.

The next day, to his surprise, he found that it was not so difficult. He still suffered, but not as much. He found himself able to concentrate better on the work. Thus, from day to day he grew more accustomed to the place and the work, until in a short time he seemed like a veteran tanner with years of experience, almost to the manner born.

Thus Scripture warns us, *and you shall not defile yourselves with them, so as to become unclean by them* (Leviticus 11:43). Do not experi-

ment or try at all to defile yourselves with non-kosher, spiritually foul
food. The first time, you will find it difficult, even revolting. You will
feel it makes you sick, almost to the point of vomiting. If someone
persists, however, then the second and third times he tries it, he begins
becoming accustomed to it. He is then already acting "so as to become
unclean by them": He is sinking into the morass of spiritual befoul-
ment, and is no longer sensitive to it....

117
TO SURVIVE HUNGER'S TEMPTATIONS

In the decades of the twentieth century, many have fallen victim to
circumstances and found themselves forced to eat non-kosher food.
Times have been hard, it has been extremely difficult to earn a living,
and food has been scarce. So it has seemed to many that if they remained strict about their meals and insisted on eating only kosher food,
they might even die of hunger. As a result, they began making allow-
ances and soon came to treat the whole matter lightly. In the beginning
they would allow themselves food that was not kosher for certain;
then they progressed to food that was definitely non-kosher, spiritually
vile for certain.

Unfortunately, there has always been the satanic evil inclination
ready to "help out" with its "good advice". It would always urge such
people on: "Look, if you hold out a long time, you may grow sick
with malnutrition, and you won't even have the stamina left to eat
and digest non-kosher food. You had better start using this other food
right now, so that you can keep your strength up until these hard times
go by." Well, such people bring to mind a parable:

A man once lost his way in the wilderness, and found himself wandering without any idea of his whereabouts. As best he could, he decided
on a direction, and started walking, hoping he would soon reach a
human settlement of some kind. Of course, he had no idea how many
days it would take before he reached some habitation of human beings.
He opened his knapsack and carefully examined the food he had left.
As he reckoned, he had only enough to last him two days — three at
the most.

In utter dismay, he sat down and gave way to despair. What should he do? What if he walked on and on for more than two or three days and still found no settlement of human beings? How would he last? How would he keep from perishing?

In his bewilderment mingled with rage and frustration, he took the bit of food he had and threw it away, down to the bottom of a ravine. "What do I need it for?" he cried. "My situation is hopeless anyway. I am never going to survive till I reach civilization. Whatever I do, I am going to die of starvation in this wilderness. Then I might as well lighten my load and have less to carry."

Of course he was criminally foolish. A man has to think very carefully before he does something that can affect his chances to survive. True, he did not have too much food left in his knapsack. True, he was in danger of dying if it took many more days before he could reach a human settlement of some kind. Still, he could have eaten his remaining food in very small rations, to make it sustain him as long as possible. And thus there was some chance, large or small, that he would succeed in his purpose. So he was an absolute fool for throwing away this chance, out of anger and worry — because this act of his sealed his fate.

Well, what of the people we have been considering? True, they found conditions difficult. Work was scarce; it was difficult to earn a decent living wage. They could barely get enough food to keep body and soul together. Perhaps there was even some chance of malnutrition and starvation.

Nevertheless, is all this a reason for a Jew to cast off the remainder of his authentic Jewish faith and observance? Is this a reason to renounce kashruth and forget about kosher food, and proceed to become spiritually foul with non-kosher food that is so abhorrent in the sight of our God?

Like the man in the wilderness, a Jew has a duty in such a case to ration his expenses and his food, and to find some way to survive until the situation eases. He has to seek help if necessary, until the blessed Lord relieves his distress and improves his lot in life. The

rescuing help of the Lord can come in the twinkling of an eye! It is
sheer lunacy to imperil our spiritual life, to expose ourselves to the
danger of spiritual death, out of the fear and anxiety of having nothing
to eat.

118
ONLY ONE MORE DAY

This is a story that the Ḥafetz Ḥayyim told to his close friends:

A Jew once found himself in the distressing situation of being away
out in the middle of nowhere, and he was forced to travel around for
many days among non-Jewish farmers and peasants. He had no way
of getting out of the region and making his way to some Jewish settlement. He had not even any money with him, with which he might buy
some permissible food from the farmers and peasants. So he was forced
to subsist on the bits of raw fruit, vegetables and water that they gave
him; and he was almost in despair at his miserable situation.

Finally, however, he managed to reach his own home, with a most
welcome sense of relief. His friends were truly glad to see him back,
and they came to talk with him about the painful experience. They
were full of curiosity.

"Is it true", one asked him, "that in all those days you had not
even one cooked dish of food or one proper meal of any kind?"

"I give you my word", he replied. "In all that time I lived on some
fruit and raw vegetables, and a little water, that they gave me. I
touched no cooked food of theirs."

"Then how were you able to keep up your strength? How is it that
you kept going without breaking down?"

"I will tell you: Quite simply, I never thought I would have to remain among them such a very long time. Every morning, having slept
in some hayloft or pile of straw, I told myself that this would surely
be my last day among the peasants. By tomorrow I would be back
in my own home. So there was only one more day to endure. Is it so
hard to bear a little suffering and discomfort for just one day? If by
the next day I could be home, would it be worth my while to become
defiled by their non-kosher cooked food, just for the sake of having

a good, enjoyable meal? The meal would be over in a very short time. The horrible effect on my spirit would last a lifetime. So I spent the day in near-starvation, making do with any bits of acceptable food I received. And that is how I went through one day after another — till at last I was really home — here, among you."

This is how a Jew must learn to think and reckon when he finds himself forced to live in the Diaspora, in a non-Jewish environment. This is how he must learn to last for the long duration without yielding to the temptation to take the forbidden food that the non-Jews consider so delicious and essential. We must be strong in our faith in the blessed Lord, trusting in Him completely, that He will hasten to rescue and liberate us from this environment. Every single day we have to reckon that it will be the last we must dwell in their midst. Tomorrow we will be home — in the true home of the Jew.

In this way the burden will be easy to bear, and there will be the inner joy of knowing that our spirit remains pure, clean and undefiled by forbidden food.

In this way, too, we can learn how to wait for the Messiah in true anticipation. Every morning we affirm that "I believe with perfect faith in the coming of the Messiah; and even if he tarries, I will nevertheless wait for him every day, expecting him to come". Let a believing Jew reckon that each and every day in the Diaspora will be the last; that tomorrow the complete and final redemption will come.

This is the attitude that has ever lightened the burden on our people through their long years in the dark and bitter exile.